THE NEXT TEST

By

MARIOS ELLINAS

All rights reserved. This book is protected by the copyright laws of the United States of America. This book may not be copied or reprinted for commercial gain or profit. The use of short quotations or occasional page copying for personal or group study is permitted and encouraged. Permission will be granted upon request.

Unless otherwise identified, all Scripture quotations are from the New King James Version. Copyright ©1982 by Thomas Nelson, Inc. Used by permission. All rights reserved.

All emphasis within Scripture quotations is the author's own. The author capitalizes certain pronouns in Scripture that refer to the Father, Son, and Holy Spirit, and may differ from some publishers' styles.

The name satan and related names are not capitalized. The author chooses not to acknowledge him, even to the point of violating grammatical rules.

For Worldwide Distribution, Printed in the U.S.A.

ISBN: 978-0-615-48252-1

The Next Test

By Marios Ellinas

Printed by Createspace

Copyright 2011 — Marios A. Ellinas

www.thenexttest.com

maellinas@yahoo.com

Cover Design by **Tulip Graphics**
tulipgr@mweb.co.za

Dedication

To my wonderful parents, Andreas and Irene Ellinas. You have taught and modeled the value of tests. Thank you for everything!

FOREWORD

This is Marios' third book. Each work contains revelation on topics all of us live through yet rarely give conclusive thoughts to what we might experience. Marios, however, causes us to reflect on our experiences, and reveals the higher purpose for the events that unfold in our lives.

Human Character demands regular testing.

In *The Next Test,* Marios takes us into a diagnostic perspective of life's Tests. Tests are an inevitable and unavoidable part of our existence in life; some we plan and prepare for while others sneak up and catch us unaware. These latter tests are the most difficult to maneuver through as we rarely get informed that "This is a test."

Maybe we would do better going through a test if we had some sort of warning, like that old black and white TV emblem that used to interrupt our cartoons as children. Anyone remember that? You would be getting into a great episode of Bugs Bunny when suddenly the black and white emblem would fill the screen accompanied by — BEEEEP — "This is a test of the emergency broadcast system. This is only a test. If this were not a test, instructions would appear on the screen indicating what you should do in case of an emergency. This is only a test — BEEEEP!!"

Do you remember how annoying that one minute long warning was? They seemed rather useless; I mean, why interrupt Bugs Bunny just to indicate a test was in progress? As a child, I did not understand the meaning of that test, and it was bothersome. Well, if we continue to remain uninformed concerning tests, they may seem like annoying interruptions which everyone is forced to endure. This is not the right attitude to have concerning tests, especially the "sneak-attack" kind.

Surprise tests never come when convenient, and they are far worse than those "pop-quizzes" we used to have in school. We can be going along on our life's journey, feeling quite on top of it all, when suddenly something shifts, and we find ourselves in a maze of choices tending to project us away from our "field of dreams".

Suddenly and without warning, questions assail us from diverse arenas of life. All too frequently, testing times are too confusing and last too long, especially for the unseasoned "testee" who doesn't have a clue as to what is happening. That is how most of these tests happen to us all — they find us clueless and throw us in a state of shock.

As you read *The Next Test*, not only will you discover some of the different conditions of testing, but you will be equipped with a readiness to discern various seasons of testing as well as find meaningful purpose in the test. The heart of Marios is to make "A" students out of all of us so that we can pass our "Next Test".

Daryl Nicolet
Sr. Leader
Faith Worship Center, Pepperell, Massachusetts

ACKNOWLEDGEMENTS

Danielle, for being my best friend and most positive influence, ever!

Christos, Caleb and Chloe, for their commitment to the assignment God has given our family. They are amazing!

My parents, Andreas and Irene Ellinas, for always speaking encouraging and empowering words over me.

Armand and Diane Chenelle, for honoring and supporting God's call on their daughter and son-in-law.

The staff and volunteers of *Valley Shore* — you make it all happen. Thanks for all your wonderful endorsements. I am honored to serve alongside you!

Mavi Nadeau, for always interceding for us. We could not prevail without her prayer-support.

Daryl Nicolet, for being an amazing friend and role model. I salute him as a general in God's Kingdom!

Every friend who made positive declarations about this book and encouraged me to keep writing.

Bethany Flugrad, Jason Hackley and Peter Sylvester, for their invaluable assistance with research, editing and formatting.

Ed Stephens and Bill Moore, for their excellent service and impeccable attitude during Valley Shore's expansion projects.

Pastor Glenn Harvison and Harvest Time Church, for generously sowing into this book project.

My teachers and mentors, whose love, instruction and example continually mold my life.

ENDORSEMENTS

It is my great pleasure to endorse Marios and *The Next Test*. I thank the Lord for Marios and how he has impacted my life. As a true apostle and a father in God's end-time army, Marios is a champion in leading mighty warriors toward their eternal destiny.

The Next Test empowers and encourages us to settle for nothing less than all our Father has for us. We discover that through tests, we learn devotion, obedience, commitment, faith, intimacy and trust. We are being prepared to rule and reign under our Father's dominion and glory.

If you have read *Running to the Impossible* and *Warrior Material*, you will love *The Next Test*. Get excited to receive victory as His will becomes your will!

William Fish
Administrator
Valley Shore Assembly of God

~ ~ ~

I have been walking with Marios since we went to Africa together and shared a room. I found there a man of God. From sunup to sundown, Marios demonstrated and shared the love of God.

Marios is a gifted minister with a remarkable knowledge of the Bible. Not only does he know God's word; he can present it in an understandable and usable form. More importantly, he lives it.

As you read *The Next Test*, you will also encounter a man who is transparent and unafraid to be real. This is not a book of do's and don'ts but a book of life. Marios does not present the gospel as a third party or an onlooker, but from his life experience. His genuineness is refreshing. As you turn the pages, you will receive impartation from a man who lives what he says and says what he lives. Enjoy!

Joseph Lynes
Children's Ministries & Extended Pastoral Team
Valley Shore Assembly of God

~ ~ ~

The Next Test is full of examples of testing, where learning is a pleasure. In a way, it will metamorphose your life.

Marios doesn't just know about tests, he has exemplified walking through them to draw us closer to the Father; to impart hope and victory at a whole different level.

Marios has a deep spiritual sensitivity, a solid biblical foundation and a heart to build the entire body of Christ. This book is a result of that!

Anthony and Sharon Signorino
Extended Pastoral Team
Valley Shore Assembly of God

~ ~ ~

Marios Ellinas is a powerfully anointed man of God. The life he leads reflects impeccable character and utmost integrity. His revelatory teaching and profound insight cause us to better understand who we are called to be as the Bride of Christ.

Marios has an innate ability to spotlight a passage of scripture and show us how to seamlessly incorporate it into our lives. He does so in such a way that it produces radical changes within us as individuals and as a body, thus bringing us into a deeper level of intimacy with our Heavenly Father.

If a divine revelation of God's truths is what you seek, then prepare to be enlightened. The words that Marios has written is evidence that he has been released to share what God has spoken to him personally. We, the Body of Christ, will surely reap the benefits of his obedience to the leading of the Holy Spirit by the writing of his third book, *The Next Test*.

Lori Cote
Head Counter
Valley Shore Assembly of God

~ ~ ~

Marios' writing and teaching engage you by letting you in on a slice of his life, which very often mirrors your own. He makes you feel like you're not alone and that if you're not perfect, it's okay.

Most of us go through life encountering periods of adversity, somehow muddling through it, and come out on the other side angry or frustrated with ourselves, with others, or even with God. We often learn little from the experience, just being relieved that it's over. However, in this book, Marios reflects on his own times of adversity and not only appreciates the lessons learned for himself, but shares those lessons in a way that will change how we view adversity. With ample references to Scripture, Marios demonstrates the purpose of these events in our lives. Instead of responding with anger and frustration, we begin to appreciate these times as lessons and testing from our Creator. We begin to realize that He won't test us beyond what we are able, and if we listen to Him, we will be far better for the experience. This is a lesson we could all use.

Michael and Debra Marino
Healing and Deliverance Ministry Team Leaders
Valley Shore Assembly of God

~ ~ ~

The book you are holding in your hands is a gift that's more precious than silver or gold. Its value will grow increasingly as you turn each page.

Marios Ellinas is a man with a wealth of Holy Spirit knowledge. His books offer useful tools, not only for everyday life but also to walk out the destiny God has in store for us. His passion for Jesus overflows into our own hearts and challenges us to become more and more like Him, in spirit and in truth.

Marios has earned the right to hand these keys to us. He has allowed the Lord to mold him through each test he has faced, going from glory to glory and walking in victory. We are excited for the reader of *The Next Test* because we know what Marios imparts is God breathed and Holy Spirit written.

We challenge you to embrace all that is written. May it stir your heart to go deeper and higher with our Lord!

Nasreen and Ed Hyde
Connect Groups Pastors
Valley Shore Assembly of God

~ ~ ~

Marios is a leader whose heart, above all, is to see God. He has a passion for His presence and an unrelenting fire to see God's kingdom come. His excitement for the impossible is contagious. I would follow him into battle no matter what.

Life is full of tests, but handling them the right way will bring extravagant breakthrough. Marios has not written this book based solely on revelation he's received; he has lived it. *The Next Test* shows vulnerability and strength that comes from someone who has a close relationship with the Lord. I'm excited to see the fruit that comes from what is written on these pages.

Bethany Flugrad
Missions Director
Valley Shore Assembly of God

~ ~ ~

I can confidently say that Marios' writing will change your life. Everything he does produces growth, provokes reformation, and establishes the government of

God on both corporate and global levels, regardless of his situation or surroundings. His fierce unrelenting desire to overcome and completely and utterly destroy adversity is nothing short of contagious and shines through in his actions and his words.

Quite frankly, Marios could write a collection of nursery rhymes for children, or a calculus textbook for college students and produce the same results — breakthrough and revival. It's who he is; it's what he lives for; and from the first chapter of *The Next Test*, it's what he's walking us through.

Patrick Lynch
Worship Pastor
Valley Shore Assembly of God

~ ~ ~

Having worked and lived life alongside Marios and his family for many years, I have witnessed and experienced many of the tests that have given him the material to write this book. I have seen Marios take many of these tests and endure challenges with grace, humility, and a teachable spirit. Now with real life experience, combined with Holy Spirit inspired revelation, Marios is able to share insight into the times of testing that we all must walk through. As you read this book, you will gain tools and keys for taking and passing tests. Get ready for promotion!

Ralene Goff
Lead Worship Pastor
Valley Shore Assembly of God

~ ~ ~

When you think about the phrase, "for such a time as this", these words explain the timing, content, and release of Pastor Marios' third book!! Those of us who are blessed to call him our Pastor can describe him as honest and totally sold out to everything that God has. Not just for himself, but for his family, the Valley Shore Family, and the world, he is as real as it gets!!

In the process of life, Pastor Marios has turned his whole heart toward God. When you go to war, which we all are in, you want a leader like Pastor. He never leads from a position being above, but from a position of being arm in arm with us!! His willingness to walk the way of The Cross, which is true holiness that intersects with true love, has caused us all to grow as we follow his lead!!

Sherry Schiavone
Minister of Maintenance
Valley Shore Assembly of God

~ ~ ~

Test. The word alone sends shivers down my spine. Though I did well in school, I never felt prepared enough when test time came. I thought I'd leave testing when I graduated school, but I've learned we are constantly being tested in one way or another. With his latest book, Pastor Marios gives us the tools we need to successfully get through life's trials. With honesty and humor, candor and scripture, Pastor Marios does what he does best: teaches us how to be better, to be stronger, to reach higher and go beyond what we think we can achieve, and he does it with love and encouragement.

Marios Ellinas has a pastor's heart that looks out for his people; a true father's heart that wants the best for his kids. And with this book, he helps us to prepare for the inevitable, The Next Test.

Mavi Nadeau
Head Intercessor
Valley Shore Assembly of God

~ ~ ~

The insight and understanding imparted through this work, *The Next Test,* can only be written from a perspective of experience and breakthrough. Pastor Marios, in this book, has shared from his own heart the very essence of character building strategies that are biblically supported and lived out. The proof is in our ability to go through the trials and come out victorious.

Thank you, Marios, for providing solid teaching and strategies that are relevant for our success. As we go through the testing and trials, *The Next Test* provides the encouragement, wisdom and understanding to help us move forward and advance the Kingdom of God.

Lydia Velez
Lead Pastor of Cancion de la Vina
Valley Shore Assembly of God

~ ~ ~

The Next Test (TNT) will blow your doors off! As a young Greek soldier, Marios was a Green Beret Special Forces demolitions expert on the Island of Cyprus, and now he's written a TNT book for the Kingdom of God. God has a sense of humor! With so many challenges to truth in our world, this book is a refreshing look at God's point of view. Marios' life is an open book and he rewards his readers with such a relatable perspective of openness and honesty. Facilitating Holy Spirit pathways from Heaven into your soul, this book will change the way you think, change the way you act, and change the way you live.

My friendship with Marios has been a very rewarding experience of love, encouragement and revelation. His role in his family, church, friendships and business relationships is conducted with impeccable integrity and honor. A man of incredible focus, he brings Glory to God and makes rich deposits into the lives of others. TNT will explode into your life, blow up the old mindsets, and release you into freedom. Read it, mark it up, digest it, and share it.

Sinco B. Steendam
Financial Bookkeeper
Valley Shore Assembly of God

~ ~ ~

Marios Ellinas is a man who walks in true Governmental Authority of the Kingdom of God. He has been tried and has come forth as gold purified by fire. He is a man who the Lord can trust with His revelations and gifts, and most important of all, a man who can be trusted with God's people. He is a man of honor who is sensitive to the leading of the Spirit and who imparts all that he is and all that he carries to everyone he meets. It is an honor to be aligned with such a man of valor and to call him Pastor.

You can rest assured that *The Next Test* will impart to you from the deep wells of the purposes of the

Kingdom that pour from Marios' life. This is his third book and I believe the Lord is using these writings to help bring His people to a maturity level unprecedented in this current season we find ourselves in.

Linda and Vinnie Santangelo
Extended Pastoral Team
Valley Shore Assembly of God

~ ~ ~

Marios has endured testing through years of battles of the mind and heart. Through it all, he has always displayed love and honor to all, a humble and teachable spirit, the joy of the Lord and strength of character. Therefore, Marios has been given keys of understanding that open doors to lead God's people to maturity.

If you want to learn how to advance and earn promotion in God's kingdom, maintain intimacy with God, and have victory in your seasons of testing, we encourage you to delve into the pages of this book, written by a man who has been tried and tested and has passed with excellence.

George and Donna Larkins
Extended Pastoral Team
Valley Shore Assembly of God

~ ~ ~

I wholeheartedly endorse this writing project. More importantly, I wholeheartedly endorse Marios, not as the author, but as a friend, and above all, my brother in Christ.

I have had the honor and privilege to serve under Marios for several years, as someone who looks after some of the responsibilities at Valley Shore but also as a disciple and 'son' in the faith. I cannot recall a time, in all the years that we've met to discuss life's tests and everything that God has in store for us, where I left one of our meetings and didn't feel like I could ace the test, being victorious throughout the entire process. Marios is a test-taker himself but he also carries some of the 'teacher edition' keys.

I enjoyed reading *The Next Test*, not only for the instruction it provides, but also because Marios saturates his work with the Word of God, which is undeniably the best writing in history. The Bible is our textbook by which we can conquer all tests. *The Next Test* is one of its companion books.

Jason Hackley
Media and IT
Valley Shore Assembly of God

~ ~ ~

The chapters in *The Next Test* read as proverbial Cliff Notes for every test you'll ever take! The words written reflect the heart of a master encourager, one who has successfully come through many tests, and believes in you!

In walking with my husband over the last sixteen years, I have learned many lessons as I have witnessed and observed Marios respond to multiple tests with integrity, honor and true character. Through my husband's example, I have learned to stand in the face of adversity and testing by walking in what I know to be my identity in Christ.

The Next Test comes from a man who is bearing abundant fruit on the other side of tests he has passed in many areas, which include family and ministry life. Anyone who has been blessed to know Marios has witnessed his heart of determination to encourage and help others press through adverse circumstances to attain victory. By reading this book, you will learn from a master how to successfully prepare for and ace your next test!

Danielle Ellinas
Wife and Co-Pastor
Valley Shore Assembly of God

Table of Contents

Introduction *23*

Chapter 1   Test Questions *31*

Chapter 2   Teachability and Testability *49*

Chapter 3   Double or Nothing *63*

Chapter 4   Crunch Time *77*

Chapter 5   Pop Quiz! *89*

Chapter 6   Test Cheats *103*

Chapter 7   The Test of Success *117*

Chapter 8   Re-Takes *131*

Chapter 9   Study Mates *147*

Chapter 10   Test Results *159*

Epilogue: The Next Test *171*

Introduction

I do not remember any time in my life when I felt as apprehensive about meeting someone as I did that November evening.

The destination programmed into my GPS device was a small town in northern Massachusetts, where my friends, Daryl and Lin, serve as the senior leaders of a thriving church. I was heading there in response to an admonition from my wife.

For several months, Danielle had watched me grit my teeth every morning and run headlong into the contrary winds of transition, challenge and adversity. A grueling expansion project for the church, the demands of a growing family and ministry, and a series of intense summer and early fall battles on various fronts took a toll on me. Though I did my best to hold it together, my wife knew I was frustrated, drained, and on edge. She was legitimately concerned, and believed Daryl would be of great help.

Daryl has served at his current post for more than twenty years. He has much experience, especially pertaining to seasons of trial. He is a remarkable pastor, a genuine friend, and a man of great wisdom. Daryl loves people unconditionally and models the Father's heart. And, he's former

The Next Test

Special Forces—a valuable common denominator in our friendship!

> It felt as though the weather and late-fall New England landscape mirrored the condition of my soul—cold, overcast and bare.

I knew my wife was right in recommending I meet with Daryl, yet it took weeks for me to warm up to the idea of reaching out for help.

My relationship with Daryl had developed through discussions of the more celebratory and triumphant aspects of our lives and ministries. In most of our previous get-togethers and phone conversations, Daryl and I had shared testimonies of how good God had been to our precious families and our beloved congregations. We had talked about miracles in people's lives and amazing Spirit-wrought transformations in our region.

I was uncomfortable with shifting into "help me" mode; more importantly, I was afraid my friend would hear my story and agree with the conclusion I had come to—I had failed as a senior leader at my current post and needed to seek a different assignment.

That Tuesday morning, in spite of all my concerns and reservations, I heeded my wife's advice and mustered the courage to call. Daryl graciously moved things around and offered to meet with me that same evening.

Introduction

My two-hour drive up to Massachusetts was unpleasant. It felt as though the weather and late-fall New England landscape mirrored the condition of my soul — cold, overcast and bare.

I pulled into the parking lot of Daryl's church around six-thirty. We embraced, exchanged greetings, and headed out to a local restaurant. We briefly caught up with each other's lives and then delved into the purpose for my visit.

Though I had resisted such a meeting for weeks, when I began to talk about things, I did my best to be thoroughly transparent and candid.

"The building project nearly wiped me out..."

"Moving into the new building has brought new, unforeseen challenges..."

"I am facing leadership issues on many fronts..."

"I am weary and vulnerable..."

"Perhaps I should consider a different assignment..."

For the most part, Daryl just listened. His large, loving eyes expressed genuine interest and deep concern. Without words, he encouraged me to keep talking. I knew he was reading me like a book, weighing everything I was saying against the internal database of knowledge, understanding and practical wisdom he had acquired over decades of leadership.

> Just like that--in one moment--all despair and disappointment left me!

By the time I was finished with my story, we were taking our last bites of the delicious three-layer chocolate cake we had ordered for dessert. Daryl asked a few questions. I answered them. Then he paused for a few moments, his eyes continually fixed on me. Having talked for so long and so openly about my troubles, I was certain a verdict of agreement with my own grim conclusions would follow.

Daryl leaned back, smiled from ear-to-ear, and said, "Wonderful...fantastic! You have done so well through your season of testing. You are ready for the next level of increase, influence, and significance!"

Immediately, something shifted inside me. I felt the same release and even joy I had felt every time I received good scores on difficult and important academic tests. Just like that - in one moment - all despair and disappointment left me!

With godly authority and the unction of the Holy Spirit, Daryl made an assessment and a declaration, which not only set me free from stress and frustration, but also propelled me into the

Introduction

wonderful season of fruitfulness and blessing that followed.

I had not lost my mind or leadership edge. I had not made calamitous decisions. No need to start packing my office just yet. I had been tested, and according to my friend who had faced and aced similar tests, I had passed. What a huge relief!

> Tests are events, circumstances, standards and processes, which evaluate various aspects of our existence.

Prior to my departure for Massachusetts earlier that day, I had booked a hotel room for a couple of nights. I expected after my meeting with Daryl I would need time alone to process things and make decisions. His profound input and my subsequent breakthrough rendered the hotel room unnecessary; therefore, I canceled my reservation and headed home.

I walked in the house around 1:30 AM. I deliberately plopped in bed loudly enough to wake up Danielle. Then I said:

"Honey, it was all a test, and we got through it. God has great things for us up ahead!"

~

I am always amazed when God's grace manifests this way! My November incident was one of many times when adverse circumstances in my life proved to be a test.

The Next Test

Tests are events, circumstances, standards and processes which evaluate various aspects of our existence, such as our identity, character, intelligence, knowledge, abilities, skills, beliefs, and values.

> Regardless of its source, timing, level of difficulty or duration, ultimately, every test and testing season has the capacity to augment our maturation and procure our advancement.

Life is replete with tests. Some tests are planned, expected, or standardized; therefore, we may study or train accordingly. Many, if not most, of life's tests are unexpected and unpredictable. It is harder to anticipate and properly prepare for the tragic loss of a loved one, relational conflicts, financial setbacks, theft, layoff, war, natural disasters, accidents or health problems.

Tests and testing seasons also vary in terms of their source, duration, magnitude and intensity. We may be tested by caring loved ones or spiteful adversaries. Some tests last for hours or days, others for weeks, months, even years. Some tests are easy; others seem impassable. Tests may cause minimal alteration from our daily routine, or they may consume a majority of our time and energy.

Regardless of its source, timing, level of difficulty or duration, ultimately, every test and testing season has the capacity to augment our maturation and procure our advancement. Tests

Introduction

prove us at levels we have already attained; passing them grants promotion to the levels we were destined to reach. Tests are integral in our development.

The Next Test examines concepts and characteristics pertaining to times and seasons of testing. I give added emphasis to tests as catalysts for positive impact and lasting benefits in our lives.

> Many of the seemingly destructive storms in our lives are indeed tests, which qualify the "seaworthiness" of our "vessels", and equip us for future voyages, explorations, and discoveries.

Many of the seemingly destructive storms we encounter are, indeed, tests which qualify the seaworthiness of our "vessels" and equip us for future voyages, explorations, and discoveries.

In that regard, tests are good, and our next test may be our best one yet!

CHAPTER 1

TEST QUESTIONS

Test Questions

~ Wise are they who have learned these truths: Trouble is temporary. Time is tonic. Tribulation is a test tube. ~

David Arthur Ward

Consider it all joy, my brethren, when you encounter various trials, knowing that the testing of your faith produces endurance. And let endurance have its perfect result, that you may be perfect and complete, lacking in nothing.

James 1:2-4

The refining pot is for silver and the furnace for gold, but the LORD tests the hearts.

Proverbs 17:2-4

A high school student walks out of the Department of Motor Vehicles, triumphantly waiving her new driver's license.

The college graduate tosses his hat in the air and then poses for pictures with the diploma.

The Trident insignia is pinned upon the Navy SEAL's chest.

A law school graduate is granted a certificate to practice law.

The Next Test

The first-place sprinter looks intensely at the stadium screen while crossing the finish line—her time qualifies her for the Olympics!

The jubilation, celebration and recognition associated with the above-mentioned accomplishments are a result of each individual's successful passage through the straits of testing.

For the new license holder, it was the written and driving exam after multiple sessions of Driver's Ed. The college student persevered through years of seminars, projects, term papers and finals. The SEAL completed 25-30 weeks of grueling Basic Underwater Demolition Training (BUDS). The lawyer passed the Bar Exam, reputedly one of the toughest tests. The sprinter endured rigorous training and edged past competitors to run the race of her life within the Olympics-qualifying timeframe.

> We rarely recognize or appreciate tests' lifelong returns or rewards *during* our times of testing.

We rarely recognize or appreciate tests' lifelong returns or rewards *during* our times of testing. Such awareness usually comes long after tests are completed and "course transcripts" or "diplomas" are issued. While we are being tested, we often resort to questioning:

Where is this challenge coming from?

Test Questions

Am I being tested for doing something wrong or right? Is this a result of failing God or is it demonic retaliation for upholding a standard of righteousness?

Do I have what it takes?

What do I do next?

When will this be over?!

Here is one of the most gnawing test-related questions, especially for Christ-followers:

What is God doing while I am being tested?

Primarily, He watches. He watches how we perceive ourselves, others, and Him during the testing season. He watches the attitude of our hearts in response to the problems we are required to solve. God watches how our character holds up and how committed we are to growing and learning through each challenge. Moreover, the Lord watches for us to trust Him, draw closer to Him, and further cultivate and strengthen our relationship.

In other words, during our times of testing, regardless of the tests' source, God watches and tests our hearts.

> *For the righteous God tests the hearts and minds.* Psalm 7:9

The Next Test

The LORD's throne is in heaven; His eyes behold, His eyelids test the sons of men. Psalm 11:3

Moses admonished the Israelites to remember how the Lord had led them for forty years in the wilderness:

"....To humble you and test you, to know what was in your heart, whether you would keep His commandments or not. Deuteronomy 8:2-3

Throughout Israel's wanderings and the subsequent conquest of Canaan, God was watching and testing people's hearts. Even after the conquest, a number of Canaanite nations remained —*"namely, five lords of the Philistines, all the Canaanites, the Sidonians, and the Hivites who dwelt in Mount Lebanon, from Mount Baal Hermon to the entrance of Hamath"* (Judges 3:3).

God "left [those] nations" for two reasons:

1. God wanted to see if, during their confrontations with the Canaanites, His people would uphold His standards, which were modeled and passed down to them by the previous generation.

"I also will no longer drive out before them any of the nations which Joshua left when he died, so that through them I

may test Israel, whether they will keep the ways of the LORD, to walk in them as their fathers kept them, or not."
Judges 2:21-22

2. God was training future generations for battle by allowing some of Israel's enemies to live in close proximity to them:

That He might test Israel by them, that is, all who had not known any of the wars in Canaan (this was only so that the generations of the children of Israel might be taught to know war, at least those who had not formerly known it)
Judges 3:1-2

Through the test of continued conflict against heathen nations, God was training generation after generation for warfare. Israel would have to physically fight both for the acquisition and preservation of their inheritance.

Many of the tests God's people face today prepare us for the warfare we must engage in to preserve *our* inheritance. However, we do not "wrestle" militarily against people groups or nations but "against principalities, against powers, against the rulers of the darkness of this age, against spiritual hosts of wickedness in the heavenly places" (Ephesians 6:12).

The Next Test

Ever since the ultimate victory Jesus obtained for us through His death on the cross and His resurrection from the grave, we do not engage in warfare in a physical way — by striving or contending in the flesh. Rather, we fight the war spiritually by resting in God, fully trusting Him, and following His Spirit to our breakthrough.

It is important to note that the Israelites' assignment in Canaan was to honor God and uphold His ways; *then*, with His help, they would "expel" the Canaanites, "drive them out" and "possess their land as the Lord your God promised." (Joshua 23:5).

Prior to his death, Joshua further admonished that God's people were not to compromise through intermarriage. He issued strong warning against such practice:

> *If indeed you do go back, and cling to the remnant of these nations – these that remain among you – and make marriages with them, and go in to them and they to you, know for certain that the LORD your God will no longer drive out these nations from before you. But they shall be snares and traps to you, and scourges on your sides and thorns in your eyes, until you perish from this good land which the LORD your God has given you.* Joshua 23:12-13

Test Questions

God's desire was for His people to possess all of Canaan through conquest. God would fight with and for the Israelites as long as they remained devoted and obedient to Him. Their loyalty to Yahweh would secure His support, and He would give Israel the victory in battle, and the land. Yet, they had to fight for it, not intermarry.

The remnants of Canaanite nations—Philistines, Sidonians, Hivites, etc. — would test the Israelites' adherence to God's directives by intimidating them out of fighting and seducing them into unholy alliances through marriage.

To honor God and secure His continued support, Israel would have to be courageous in battle and resolute against intermarriage. Such testing, and the opportunity for complete takeover of the land (a test which Israel failed), could not have been possible if all the Canaanites had been driven out during Joshua's time. In other words, the only way God could prove His people's devotion and obedience was through the test posed by the remaining heathen nations.

God wants us to conquer enemy territory and advance His Kingdom. He will fight for us if we pass the same tests of devotion and obedience. Therefore, just as in the case of generations of Israelites in Canaan, He allows or even arranges conditions of conflict,

> God's testing of our hearts is by no means confined to times of conflict.

which test our Christian commitment and faith. Then He watches how we perform on those tests.

God's testing of our hearts is by no means confined to times of conflict. He is *always* testing our hearts, whether we feel we are being tested or not. When we are not being tested through adverse circumstances, a different kind of testing ensues, that of honoring God and remaining faithful to Him through times of success, peace and prosperity.

This truth is illustrated in the Bible through an excerpt from the life of Solomon:

Following the completion of the construction projects for his own house and the temple of God, King Solomon and the nation of Israel entered into a season of unprecedented peace and phenomenal prosperity. Solomon's fame and influence was widespread, as he was recognized both nationally and internationally for his wisdom. Israel was respected for its wealth and power. This was undoubtedly the greatest moment of the king and his kingdom:

> *King Solomon surpassed all the kings of the earth in riches and wisdom. And all the kings of the earth sought the presence of Solomon to hear his wisdom, which God had put in his heart...So he reigned over all the kings from the River[g] to the land of the Philistines, as far as the border of Egypt. The king made silver as*

> *common in Jerusalem as stones, and he made cedar trees as abundant as the sycamores which are in the lowland. And they brought horses to Solomon from Egypt and from all lands.*
> 2 Chronicles 9:22-23, 26-28

Perhaps the greatest blessing was being able to enjoy such prosperity and influence within a context of peace from war.

As in the case of the Israelites in Canaan, Solomon's father, David, had encountered and passed numerous tests of military conflict, both within and outside Israel. He frequently fought wars with neighboring nations, he continually contended with the Philistines, and he was forced to quell several rebellions in Israel, including that of his own son, Absalom.

From as far back in David's life as the record shows, David approached all tests of conflict from a place of intimacy with God and complete trust in Him.

With a few unfortunate exceptions—for which God's grace still proved sufficient—David honored the Lord. He worshipped God passionately and sought His counsel and direction in his endeavors. Consequently, God richly blessed David with anointing, wisdom, wealth, spiritual leaders, mighty warriors, competent administrators, and everything else necessary for victory at home and abroad.

The Next Test

After forty years as king and a full life of growing in God through various tests and trials, David passed on, leaving Solomon a kingdom that was ideally primed for dominion and glory. Moreover, a wonderful generational blessing was locked in through the remarkable relationship David developed with God during his times of testing. Consequently, God promised Solomon a reign without the strife, wars, rebellions, famines, and losses David had to endure.

> As long as Solomon remained committed to God, he would enjoy the peace and prosperity David had brokered.

As long as Solomon remained committed to God, he would enjoy the peace and prosperity David had brokered.

> *As for you, if you walk before Me as your father David walked, and do according to all that I have commanded you, and if you keep My statutes and My judgments, then I will establish the throne of your kingdom, as I covenanted with David your father…*
> 2 Chronicles 7:17-18

Solomon did not fare well without tests of adversity. The abundance of material possessions and the prominence Solomon enjoyed within the context of peace and tranquility led him away from God. Interestingly, Solomon's disobedience and disloyalty toward God manifested (once again) in the form of unholy alliances with heathen nations through marriage:

> *King Solomon loved many foreign women...women of the Moabites, Ammonites, Edomites, Sidonians, and Hittites – from the nations of whom the LORD had said to the children of Israel, "You shall not intermarry with them, nor they with you. Surely they will turn away your hearts after their gods."*
> 1 Kings 11:1-2

The more Solomon "clung to [his] seven hundred wives, princesses, and three hundred concubines" (1 Kings 11:3), the farther his heart was drawn away from God.

> *For it was so, when Solomon was old, that his wives turned his heart after other gods; and his heart was not loyal to the LORD his God, as was the heart of his father David.* 1 Kings 11:4

God was angry with Solomon and pronounced judgment on him and the nation. With the exception of one tribe—Judah—which would be preserved and given to Solomon's son for David's sake(!), Israel would be "torn" out of the hand of Solomon and handed over to his servant Jeroboam.

The Next Test

> Many of life's tests are unavoidable; however, repeats of certain tests are unnecessary.

The next few verses after the pronouncement are significant:

> *Now the LORD raised up an adversary against Solomon, Hadad the Edomite*
> 1 Kings 11:14

> *And God raised up another adversary against him, Rezon the son of Eliadah*
> 1 Kings 11:23

> *Then Solomon's servant, Jeroboam the son of Nebat, an Ephraimite from Zereda, whose mother's name was Zeruah, a widow, also rebelled against the king.* 1 Kings 11:26

Solomon's failure to honor God during a time of peace took Israel to the place of being tested by internal and external conflict all over again.

Many of life's tests are unavoidable; however, repeats of certain tests are unnecessary. We are most prone to question God's commitment and support when our decisions and actions result in our having to repeat tests God already saw us through. We will be examining this concept more extensively in an upcoming chapter.

~

Test Questions

I often face tests that are overwhelming, especially at the outset. On certain days, two or three different crises can appear out of nowhere, almost simultaneously. One particular day, at the outset of a staff meeting in which we had to work with our team to find solutions for pressing church problems, Danielle and I received a call from our children's school. One of our boys had misbehaved. We were asked to meet with the principal as soon as possible. We rushed out of the meeting, wondering what on earth could have taken place. On our way to the school, the "Brake" light came on in our car, indicating the need for repairs. Within less than an hour, we found ourselves juggling several testing issues at once!

I believe everyone has faced a similar scenario or two. Troublesome circumstances emerge, closely followed by discouragement, disappointment, self-pity and other subversive spirits seeking entry. Without the right attitude, especially at the outset of a test, the impact of our trials can become widespread. Asking the right questions, while avoiding the wrong ones, maximizes our potential for overcoming.

I offer the following practical tools for handling questions that may arise during times of testing:

> First, determine not to ask where the test is coming from (God or the enemy). Knowing God is testing our hearts through every

situation, we must focus on the attitude of our hearts, rather than the source of the test.

Secondly, do not ask any "Why" questions:

- "Why is this happening to me?"
- "Why is this not happening to someone else?"
- "Why is this happening to me right now?"

God does not answer "Why" questions *during* a test. The source and purpose for a test, as well as the Lord's hand in bringing us through, usually come into focus when the test is far behind us.

Thirdly, approach the issues at hand with "What" and "How" questions:

- "How should I pray?"
- "How can I respond?"
- "How do I apply what I've learned to what I'm facing?"
- "What should be my very next move?"
- "What does God's Word say about my situation?"
- "What does my past indicate regarding God's faithfulness in times of crisis?"
- "What will the Lord do this time to turn what may be meant for evil, for my benefit?"

Test Questions

The most important "test-related" question is not, "What is God's part in this?" or "Where is God when we need Him?" Rather, will *we* prove ourselves faithful, and continually grow in Christ, regardless of our circumstances? Will we properly align ourselves with God's thoughts and heart, and avoid unnecessary failures, battles and repeats of previous tests?

Our heavenly Father is watching and testing our hearts through all seasons and circumstances. As His eyes "run to and fro throughout the whole earth", (2 Chron. 16:9) He searches for hearts that are fully loyal to him, both through hardship and trouble, as well as success and prosperity. For those who have such hearts, there is never a shortage of divine intervention, no matter what the test may be!

CHAPTER 2

TEACHABILITY AND TESTABILITY

Teachability and Testability

~ "The test of leadership is not to put greatness into humanity, but to elicit it, for the greatness is already there" ~

President James Buchanan

Teachability is the willingness and aptitude to learn. "Testablility" is the willingness and aptitude to encounter and surmount tests, as part of the learning process. Learning and testing are directly related. The more we learn, the more tests we undergo. Whenever we engage an educational process to acquire new information, knowledge, skills or experience, we essentially sign up for tests. Continual learning necessitates continual testing. The degree to which we grow is subject to our teachability, which in turn, hinges on our testability. These two growth factors go hand in hand.

College students, for example, enroll in courses to obtain the knowledge, skills or experience (and academic credits) necessary for progression to the next stage of their development i.e. subsequent courses and degrees, or a career. Periodic tests evaluate students' retention and understanding of the material presented in class.

Consider an imaginary syllabus of a class in Cell Biology. The brief description of the course would be followed by a section outlining the course's objectives, reading as such:

COURSE OBJECTIVES

Through this course, students will:

- Understand various cellular processes.
- Think analytically and strengthen problem - solving skills.
- Effectively read and comprehend assigned scientific literature.
- Appreciate how the understanding of cell biology has resulted in medical advances.

Next on the syllabus would be an explanation of the course requirements:

GRADING

- Each student's percent score will be computed based on the following scale:

Exam 1: 20 %

Exam 2: 20 %

Exam 3: 20 %

Final Exam: 25 %

5 quizzes: 15 %

• Letter grades will be assigned according to the following scale:

PERCENT SCORE GRADE

≥ 90 A

80 – 89 B

70 – 79 C

60 – 69 D

≤ 60 F

From the very outset of this course devised for the purposes of illustration, students would be made aware of what would be taught, as well as how they would be tested on the material. Three tests and five quizzes would be administered after portions of the course were presented in class. The final exam would test material from the entire semester. Then, grades would be assigned according to the students' scores on tests and quizzes.

> Most, if not all, new knowledge we obtain gets assessed and substantiated by tests.

Passing the course to fulfill the requirement for a major in biology or graduation altogether would depend on how students fare on tests. This fictional course represents an academic reality:

Testing is often chosen as the most effective and reliable means by which instructors and institutions assess student progress.

In school, tests follow teaching. It works that way in many areas of life. Most, if not all, new knowledge we obtain gets assessed and substantiated by tests.

The knowledge and insight Danielle and I gained in child-rearing during the infant and toddler stages of our first son were put to the test when our second son went through the same stages. Everything we learned from raising the first two children was exceptionally tested when our daughter came!

If we are being tested, it means we are growing and maturing. During times of testing, it is important to maintain a good attitude and right perspective about tests, because the rigor and discomfort of tests can take a toll on our passion to learn; hence, our capacity to grow.

The Bible tells us to "Cast [our] burden on the Lord and He shall sustain [us]" (Psalm 55:22). When we cast all our trials to God, He applies His grace to any vestiges of fear, stress, torment, disappointment, discouragement, pain or frustration associated with our testing circumstances.

Teachability and Testability

Consequently, the scars from past seasons of trial are covered over by God's grace.

When tests are filtered through the sieves of God's grace, the negative elements of our trials are extracted, leaving our passion and hunger for growth unhindered; thus, we maintain teachability.

~

In our world, various tests are designed to lead us to the next level with everything we need to succeed at that level. Through our test preparation and overall experience in the testing process, we obtain the knowledge, skill, and character required for effectiveness at the new level.

A construction project involves numerous "layers" of assembly and composition, each of which is qualified by an inspection. Inspections are essentially tests which ensure the integrity of construction up to a certain point. For instance, the foundation inspection evaluates the soundness of the concrete slab, upon which the rest of the building will be erected. The "test" ensures the foundation is sturdy enough to handle the weight of all subsequent construction—the frame, roof, walls, etc.

Driving tests are designed to ensure student drivers have the knowledge and skills necessary to properly operate a vehicle on the road.

The Next Test

Entrance exams test candidates' foundational knowledge in the field of study they seek to move into (nursing, teaching, medicine, law, etc.).

Similarly, life's trials, such as relational conflict, protracted illness or financial loss, instill in us the qualities necessary for significance in forthcoming levels. Our ultimate objective is to be like Jesus, having a heart that attracts and releases the glory of God in this world:

> *Beloved, do not think it strange concerning the fiery trial which is to try you, as though some strange thing happened to you; but rejoice to the extent that you partake of Christ's sufferings, that when His glory is revealed, you may also be glad with exceeding joy.*
> 1 Peter 4:12

~

Proper positioning makes a big difference. A college senior who spends a large portion of her last semester interning with a firm will be positioned for an entry-level job upon graduation. A young apprentice of a childless, middle-aged carpenter is positioned for taking over the business when the carpenter retires. A young adult who saved her allowance and summer job pay since childhood is positioned for paying college tuition without incurring debt or making a significant initial investment in stocks.

Teachability and Testability

Danielle and I occasionally get to have fun with the concept of being "positioned properly" at wedding receptions to receive the maximum benefit from the warm hors d'oeuvres being distributed by servers who walk among the guests while the wedding party is taking pictures. We watch for the "trajectory" of the various delicacy-laden trays and position ourselves appropriately to receive.

> Proper positioning in our walk with God stems from devotion and intimacy.

On a more serious note, yet applying the same principle, it is important to recognize how the Spirit of God is moving at different times and to position ourselves in His flow. Whether it is our personal lives, families, cities, regions or nations, God is continually moving and speaking. Through our relationship with Jesus, we must recognize what the Spirit is saying and doing, then position ourselves to receive and release His life-transforming words and initiatives.

Proper positioning in our walk with God stems from devotion and intimacy. In the "secret place" or the prayer closet, we recognize and have the opportunity to align with God's will and purposes. It is as though our times with Him tune our ears to the "frequency" which continually broadcasts the Lord's nature, His ways and His directives.

Heaven's frequency and the voice of the Spirit are not audible in the natural; neither can the movements of God be seen with the eye at all times. We must approach everything "pertaining to life and godliness" by faith, including proper positioning, to be a conduit of God's blessings.

On any battlefield, the best position for an army is "the high ground." Over the course of history, millions of soldiers have made the ultimate sacrifice while trying to defend or occupy advantageous posts on hills or mountains.

On the spiritual battleground to which each of us has been assigned by the Lord of Hosts, the best positioning is found between two attitudes of the heart: First, recognition, gratitude, and praise for everything God has already accomplished in and through our lives. Secondly, a relentless pursuit of the amazing, unimaginable things yet to come — heavenly blessings "eye has not seen nor ear heard", but which God has made available to His children by revealing them to us "through His Spirit." (1 Corinthians 2:9, 10)

The first attitude requires a thankful heart and appreciation for every "day of small beginnings." The second hinges on staying humble and teachable. Teachability fosters the acquisition of new knowledge, ability, insight and experience; it also precipitates tests, which brings us back to the concept of *testability*.

Testability is influenced by internal and external factors. Personal dedication to our growth process and the working of the Spirit in our lives are internal factors; instruction and guidance from mentors or teachers are external.

I ascribe great value to mentoring relationships. Proper learning and preparation for life's tests are contingent upon more than the passing of information from teacher to student; it requires an impartation of one's life to another through relationships much like those intended for parents and children. The Apostle Paul addressed this dynamic in his first letter to the church of Corinth:

> *For though you might have ten thousand instructors in Christ, yet you do not have many fathers; for in Christ Jesus I have begotten you through the gospel. Therefore I urge you, imitate me.*
> 1 Corinthians 4:15-16

Paul makes a similarly passionate declaration in his letter to the Thessalonians:

> *So, being thus tenderly and affectionately desirous of you, we continued to share with you not only God's good news (the Gospel) but also our own lives as well, for you had become so very dear to us.*
> 1 Thessalonians 2:8 (Amplified Bible)

The Next Test

During my college years, I often heard friends and classmates say, "Don't choose courses; choose professors." Good counsel! — especially as it pertained to high-level history courses, in which the class was comprised of only a handful of students.

> The most effective learning atmospheres are not established when teachers teach what they know; rather, when teachers impart who they are through the process of sharing life with their students.

Every professor within my department had remarkable knowledge and understanding of history. If I had just wanted to obtain information, learn how to write papers, take tests and obtain academic credits, I would have chosen any one of the courses at random. In that case, I would have been choosing with my mind. In the depths of my soul, however, was a longing for more; a longing that drove me to choose courses with my heart.

I "took" professors who could teach history in a way that made the subject alive, exciting and relevant. I learned from teachers who had the discernment and perception to recognize the spark of inspiration in their students, and who cared enough to impact our lives beyond the classroom. I took courses with professors who carried contagious, life-transforming DNA on the inside. I found two professors, as such, and took every

Teachability and Testability

course they offered. My last forty history credits came from courses taught by those two men.

The most effective learning atmospheres are not established when teachers teach what they know; rather, when teachers impart who they are through the process of sharing life with their students.

Protégés, who live with an insatiable passion to grow and learn, put a demand on their mentors for training and education that flows from a fathering/mothering relationship. Over time, as they work through the mentoring process with an attitude of respect, service and honor toward their mentors, protégés receive impartation that takes them to greater levels of teachability and testability.

Then, the process is repeated when protégés become mentors, and continue the same model of discipleship. May we apply these principles to all mentoring and discipleship in which we participate!

> *And the things that you have heard from me among many witnesses, commit these to faithful men who will be able to teach others also.* 2 Timothy 2:2

The Next Test

CHAPTER 3

DOUBLE OR NOTHING

~ **clear·ance** (klîr'əns)

1. The act or process of clearing.
2. A space cleared; a clearing.
3. a. The amount of space or distance by which a moving object clears something.
b. The height or width of a passage: *an underpass with a 13-foot clearance.*
4. An intervening space or distance allowing free play, as between machine parts.
5. Permission for an aircraft, ship, or other vehicle to proceed, as after an inspection of equipment or cargo or during certain traffic conditions.

6. Official certification of blamelessness, trustworthiness, or suitability. (emphasis mine)

7. A sale, generally at reduced prices, to dispose of old merchandise.
8. The passage of checks and other bills of exchange through a clearing-house.
9. *Physiology*
    a. The removal by the kidneys of a substance from blood plasma.
    b. Renal clearance.

The American Heritage Dictionary

During my time of military service, I came to understand the concept of "clearance" as it pertains to authorization.

Whenever I had night duty, one of my responsibilities was to patrol the perimeter of the base, inspecting among other things the condition of a number of storage units. I was required to walk around each storage unit and test the

The Next Test

padlocks to the doors. Once I determined the doors were properly locked, I would sign a logbook at each location.

After more than two years of service at the same base and hundreds of patrol rounds and signatures, I had not seen the inside of one of those storage units. One day toward the end of my conscription, a good friend of mine was selected by an officer to move items from one storage unit to another.

Seeing an opportunity to find out what lay behind the padlocked steel doors, I walked up to the threshold of the unit where my friend was working. Before I could open the door widely enough to take a peek inside, the hoarse voice of the officer supervising the operation stopped me dead in my tracks:

"You have no clearance to be here. Leave immediately!"

I asked my friend about the storage units when he returned from his duties. He said he worked inside two of them all day, handling wooden boxes, but did not know of their contents. We never discovered what lay in those boxes. My clearance only extended to the inspection of the exterior of the storage units; my friend's clearance proved to be limited as well.

The storage units were only one of many restricted areas within our Special Forces combat unit. With the exception of a handful of high-ranking officers who had unlimited access, everyone had clearance restrictions.

In the military, government, business and numerous other sectors of society, individuals are granted clearance or authorization for certain areas and/or information, depending on their rank, position, or sphere of responsibility.

A person's place in any given sector involves trust. Beyond qualifications, skills, education and experience, people's access to and operation in various posts depends on their trustworthiness. Advancement to greater levels of authority, responsibility and influence hinges on trust as well.

> Trust grows through trial. The more difficult the test, the more trust we earn when we overcome.

Trust cannot be fabricated or purchased. No one can force others to trust him/her. A person's trust must be earned.

Trust is integral to life and service within God's kingdom. The depth of our relationships (especially with God), the extent of our influence, and the measure of our authority will always be proportional to the degree of trust we earn.

Trust grows through trial. The more difficult the test, the more trust we earn when we overcome. The more God can trust us, the more He entrusts to us.

The Next Test

In other words, certain upgrades or promotions for us require upgrades of character in us, especially in the area of trust. The best trust-upgrades usually follow the worst trials.

The biblical account of Job's life presents one of the most extensive and intense stories of suffering ever recorded.

Job was a citizen from the land of Uz. He was the most wealthy and influential man in the land, but also the most righteous and faithful. Job loved God and honored Him in all his ways. At about the middle of the first chapter, Job's wonderful life takes a sudden turn downhill:

Within the span of a few hours, messengers brought Job horrific news: His oxen and sheep were stolen by raiders. His servants were slaughtered. Lightning struck his sheep and their caretakers. Job's camels were stolen and the servants assigned to the camels were killed. Moreover, all Job's sons and daughters perished when a strong wind caused the house where they were feasting to collapse over them.

Not long after that dreadful day in his life, Job's health was attacked. He was struck with boils "from the sole of his foot to the crown of his head" (Job 2:7). Through all these trials, Job found no support from his wife:

> *Then his wife said to him, "Do you still hold fast to your integrity? Curse God and die!"* Job 2:9

Job's friends who came to visit him were of no help either. One after another, the "friends" took turns criticizing and sermonizing Job, citing his sinfulness as the reason for his plight.

Job experienced protracted, extreme trial.

While reading through the book of Job some time ago, I came upon a very puzzling verse. It is found in the last chapter:

> *Then all his brothers, all his sisters, and all those who had been his acquaintances before, came to him and ate food with him in his house; and they consoled him and comforted him for all the adversity that the LORD had brought upon him. Each one gave him a piece of silver and each a ring of gold.* Job 42:11

The words, "for the adversity that the LORD had brought upon him" stunned me! The *Lord* brought this adversity on Job?!

Just to make sure I was not off-base, I went back to the beginning of the book and re-read the first two chapters. What I read validated my astonishment. God was neither the producer nor the director of the "reality horror flick" Job's life portrays. God did not orchestrate and execute the annihilation of Job's offspring, herds and servants. God did not give Job boils; and neither did He have anything to do with Job's wife and friends' inappropriate responses to his sufferings. As the next few paragraphs indicate, all the trouble in Job's life was satan's doing (*please note my disclaimer on the copyright page regarding the non-capitalization of the enemy's name*).

At a time when God held Job in the most high esteem, asserting "there is none like him on the earth, a blameless and upright man, one who fears God and shuns evil" (Job 1:8), satan claimed Job's allegiance to God was circumstantial and conditional:

> *Satan answered the LORD and said, "Does Job fear God for nothing? Have You not made a hedge around him, around his household, and around all that he has on every side? You have blessed the work of his hands, and his possessions have increased in the land. But now, stretch out Your hand and touch all that he has, and he will surely curse You to Your face!* Job 1:9-11

God then granted satan permission to strike:

> *And the LORD said to satan, "Behold, all that he has is in your power; only do not lay a hand on his person."* Job 1:12

After the first round of devastation and loss, Job, though broken and sorrowful, proved God right:

> *He fell to the ground and worshiped. And he said: "Naked I came from my mother's womb, and naked shall I return there. The LORD gave, and the LORD has taken away; blessed be the name of the LORD." In all this, Job did not sin nor charge God with wrong.* Job 1:20-22

The next time God and satan met, the Lord referred to Job's "high score" on the previous test:

> *And still he holds fast to his integrity, although you incited Me against him, to destroy him without cause."* Job 2:3

The enemy was relentless:

> *So satan answered the LORD and said, "Skin for skin! Yes, all that a man has he will give for his life. But stretch out Your hand now, and touch his bone and his flesh, and he will surely curse You to Your face!"* Job 2:5

Again, divine permission was granted:

> *"Behold, he is in your hand, but spare his life."*

Satan left the presence of the Lord (he could not touch God's children in His presence!); then

The Next Test

Job was struck with boils, and thirty-five more chapters of misery followed.

The record makes it abundantly clear: satan was the source of Job's sufferings, not God.

If God did not cause all the trouble in Job's life, why does the verse toward the end of the book state Job's relatives came to comfort Job for the adversity "that the LORD had brought upon Him"?

Even the Lord Himself, after the first round of satanic attacks, referred to the matter by telling satan, "you incited Me against him!" It is also very interesting to note the lightning which burned up Job's sheep is referred to as "the fire of God [which] fell from Heaven" (Job 1:16), when, clearly, satan was behind all the devastation the lightning caused.

So why is a good God, who respects and commends Job, directly implicated in Job's sufferings?

The answer is found in the last few verses in the book of Job, particularly verse 10:

> *And the LORD restored Job's losses...indeed the LORD gave Job twice as much as he had before.* Job 42:10

God also added to Job's double portion of possessions seven sons, three beautiful daughters, one hundred and forty more years of life and four generations of grandchildren (Job 42:12-13, 15-16).

When satan approached God and proposed a test of Job's devotion and loyalty, his sinister intent was to defame and destroy Job. God, on the other hand, saw the hellish test as an opportunity to bless Job with double; therefore, He assumed responsibility for all the evil satan brought upon Job. God knew Job could be trusted. Once Job's trust was proven through the test, God would grant Job more...*clearance*.

The restoration of Job's health and the increase God brought to his family and material possessions are undoubtedly significant rewards for passing the test. The most lasting blessing was influence. The new level of clearance enabled Job to influence future generations, all the way to this very moment, with his example of perseverance and steadfastness to the Truth.

If Job was "the greatest of all the people of the East" (Job 1:3) at the beginning of the story, imagine how powerful and influential he became with double what he had before, while still maintaining the integrity and uprightness for which he had been commended by God all along!

Centuries after the story of Job had been written, the Apostle James, while commending

The Next Test

God's prophets who had persevered through much trial, confirmed once again God's motive in the episode with Job:

> *Indeed we count them blessed who endure. You have heard of the perseverance of Job and seen the end intended by the Lord — that the Lord is very compassionate and merciful.*
> James 5:11

The "end intended by the Lord" was to increase Job's wealth, power and influence. Job's integrity and enduring faith throughout his trials gave God the opportunity He was looking for all along. He beat the enemy in his own game, restored Job, and lavished His servant with outrageous blessings.

~

Tests are not always packaged as tests. What we may perceive as opposition, demonic attack, personal failure, or loss, may be the very trial that launches us into wonderful and glorious realms of blessing, service and influence God intends for us to experience.

God is not responsible for much of the trouble people ascribe to His Name, especially as it pertains to sickness, natural disasters, violence, and premature death. Those are not the works of God; rather, they are the works of the enemy.

> God will leverage every satanic attack for our benefit and the advancement of His Kingdom, when we continue to draw close to Him and trust Him through the trial.

Insurance companies are mistaken in referring to earthquakes, floods, tornadoes and hurricanes as "acts of God." Instead of associating God with the disasters, we should honor Him for what He does to touch lives during and after such events. His comfort and grace for the victims, as well as His faithfulness in the restoration process, are the true acts of God.

Although God may not initiate certain tests in our lives, He assumes full responsibility, knowing He will "work all things for good." God will leverage every satanic attack for our benefit and the advancement of His Kingdom, when we continue to draw close to Him and trust Him through the trial. As we successfully pass through the testing grounds of attack, persecution or opposition at any given level, God grants to us increased authority (clearance) at that particular level. We are then able to help others who face similar challenges. Moreover, from any level we attain, we obtain access to greater levels, yet.

I close the chapter with three verses I always draw from during times of testing:

> *Let my vindication come from Your presence; Let Your eyes look on the things that are upright. You have tested*

The Next Test

my heart; You have visited me in the night; You have tried me and have found nothing; I have purposed that my mouth shall not transgress. Psalm 17:2-4

CHAPTER 4

CRUNCH TIME

> *~ Success always comes when preparation meets opportunity ~*
> Henry Hartman

The gospels of Matthew and Luke record a teaching in which Jesus likened the person who hears His words and "does them" to a man who built his house on a rocky foundation (Luke 6:48).

Conversely, a person who hears the Lord's teachings, but "did nothing" is like a man who built a house "on the sand" (Matthew 7:26), "without a foundation" (Luke 6:49).

Both homes experienced a storm. As "the rain descended, the floods came, and the winds blew and beat on" the two houses, the house built on the rock withstood the forces of the storm; whereas the house built on the sand collapsed (Luke 6:47-49).

The builder whose house withstood the forces of nature had recognized early in the building process the significance of building in a way that would prepare his house for storms. In other words, preparation for the test from the forces of nature had to be made during construction—long before the storms came. Consequently, the builder paid the necessary price in time, hard labor and expense to dig deep and build on a rock, so as to best prepare the house for impending tests.

The Next Test

The best time to prepare for war is during times of peace.

Oftentimes, we face tests which are sudden and unpredictable. I liken them to the pop-quizzes that often haunt students in academia. Planned or methodical preparation for such tests is difficult. The next chapter offers suggestions in coping with life's pop-quizzes. The purpose of the present chapter is to examine tests for which we have advance notice, emphasizing the forms and advantages of preparation.

I occasionally watch one of the numerous "Cooking Shows" on television. Such programs generally feature a chef or group of chefs, who demonstrate to a live audience and TV viewers how to cook or bake various dishes. Some of the chefs' culinary creations are spectacular—my appetite always gets a boost, and so does my desire to cook.

After comparing my actual experiences in the kitchen with the content of the cooking shows, I have reached the conclusion that the TV chefs make cooking look easier and more enjoyable than it is for the average "weekend warrior" cook. One major difference is found in the area of preparation.

Chefs have the finest pots, pans, serving dishes, ovens, stoves, gadgets, spices, condiments, meats, vegetables, marinades, etc. at their disposal.

Crunch Time

All necessary recipe ingredients and kitchenware, down to the last utensil, are meticulously lined up by the chefs or their staffs before filming begins.

My own cooking-show-inspired efforts to produce the Stuffed Chicken Cordon-bleus and the triple-layered Chocolate Mousse Towers quickly revealed the significance of preparation. Here are some of my preparation considerations, which are already in place when the TV chefs walk on the set:

- Making a list of all necessary ingredients for the recipe.
- Driving to the store, parking and obtaining a shopping cart.
- Pushing the cart through the store aisles to purchase the items.
- Waiting in line to pay for groceries.
- Loading groceries in the car.
- Driving home.
- Unloading the bags.
- Finding and setting up all necessary utensils in my kitchen (with far less room and ambiance than the TV set kitchen).
- Cutting, shredding, mincing or grinding all food items to meet recipe specifications.
- Washing, drying, and storing all pots, pans, gadget attachments and utensils used.

The Next Test

> The more diligently and thoroughly we prepare for tasks and assignments, the greater our ease during performance. Adequate preparation facilitates effective execution.

After hours of preparation, I am barely at a level playing field with the cooking show chefs, not to mention the occasional omission of an ingredient or the absence of necessary utensils, requiring my return to the store.

Each bowl of chopped onions or sliced peppers TV chefs gracefully empty into their frying pans requires much preparatory work. I propose the chief reason why cooking may seem to be easy on the shows is the preparation done by production crews beforehand.

The more diligently and thoroughly we prepare for tasks and assignments, the greater our ease during performance. Adequate preparation facilitates effective execution. Putting in the time and effort to prepare for some of life's tests can make a big difference with the feel of certain tests, as well as their results.

I don't believe any mother will deny pregnancy and childbirth is a test. The nine-month process and especially the delivery can be very challenging. During her first pregnancy, my wife was able to attend a series of *Lamaze* classes, in preparation for childbirth. During the sessions, Danielle was instructed on many birth-related topics. She watched videos of women in childbirth. She learned various relaxing and breathing techniques. She was taught to stay focused. One class was devoted to nursing. Danielle appreciated the Lamaze preparation because it helped her know what to expect and what to do at different times during her "test." Childbearing was undoubtedly difficult, but Danielle's preparation helped a lot.

Test preparation is positively influenced by two factors:

1. Realistic expectation of what the test requires of us.
2. Vision for the test's benefits.

The writing process of my books illustrates the first factor.

Each of my publications has tested me similarly in some areas, and uniquely in other areas. My preparation for writing the first book included compiling written material, saving funds, purchasing domain names and serial book numbers, coordinating various professionals who would aid with design, editing, formatting, etc., and a host of other tasks.

Preparation helped me significantly; however, the task of publishing for the first time posed some unexpected challenges. As I worked through the various steps, I developed more accurate and realistic expectations of the writing and publishing process.

The insight I received while working on *Running to the Impossible* helped me to prepare better for writing my second book, *Warrior Material*.

Nonetheless, I still faced some new challenges with the second book. For instance, I got hit with a severe case of "writer's block", which lasted for two months. Mid-book, I simply felt I had nothing further to say. It was a very difficult time, but God came through for me. I had several dreams and encounters, by which He encouraged me to keep writing. He then "downloaded" fresh revelation. Once the block lifted, I completed the rest of the book in a month.

Shortly after passing the *Warrior Material* test, I began preparations for this current work. The experiences of the first two books increasingly improved my insight regarding the challenges I should expect and prepare for with *The Next Test*. Even so, this book has proved to be a different testing ground altogether. Perhaps I will share more about the challenges of this particular project in the future.

Although we may be unable to fully prepare for the unique challenges of each assignment, the more realistic our expectation of what lies ahead, the better we can prepare.

Vision toward positive results can be another important element in our preparation for the tests that lie between us and our accomplished missions. Vision is what moves us forward, especially during times of trial. We set our eyes on the goal and press toward it.

My preparation for each of the writing projects was influenced immensely by my hope and vision for the books' long-term impact within many faith movements, both nationally and internationally. For instance, in my preparation for requesting endorsements from friends and co-laborers, I gave serious consideration to the spiritual background, Kingdom assignment and character of every person I would ask. The broader the spectrum represented by the books' endorsers, the closer I would get to the fulfillment of my vision.

Vision toward beneficial test results also helps us prepare mentally, emotionally and/or spiritually for the rigors of upcoming tests. The Apostle Paul had a God-inspired vision to bear witness of God at Rome, as he had also "testified of [Him] in Jerusalem" (Acts 23:11). Paul's vision helped him prepare his heart and body for the astounding opposition, rejection, persecution, and suffering he would experience en route to Rome.

~

We have discussed preparation *for* tests; now we will look into preparation *from* tests. Some tests are easy and some are hard. In terms of personal

The Next Test

comfort, being tested is certainly harder than not being tested at all. Whether we have an opportunity to prepare for it or not, every test carries potential to prepare *us* for what lies ahead.

The preparation we undergo during times of testing can often be as valuable or even of greater value than the actual rewards for passing the tests. A season in David's life provides an illustration of this point.

Shortly after David killed Goliath and led Israel into victory against the Philistines, he found himself serving King Saul, both as an officer in the army and the king's personal "worship leader." David's passion, courage, skills and character distinguished him in every area of service to the king. Soon, Saul became jealous of David and began to persecute him.

The last twelve chapters of the book of 1 Samuel record twenty-one attempts against David's life by King Saul. During that time, David was tested significantly. Beyond running for his life due to the constant threat posed by Saul and his armies, David faced a score of other trials:

- The temporary loss of his wife, Michal, and the permanent loss of Jonathan's companionship (1 Samuel 19 & 20).
- His unfortunate implication with Saul's massacre of all the priests, families, and livestock at Nob (1 Samuel 22).

- Frequent leadership challenges associated with David's leadership over four hundred renegades who joined ranks with him in the cave of Adullam.
- The temptation to kill Saul when David had the opportunity to do so twice, while being hunted down by the king (1 Samuel 24 & 26).
- Nabal's offense, which enraged David's and almost led to his shedding of innocent blood in revenge (1 Samuel 25).
- The ethical dilemma and manifold challenges involved with posing as an ally of the Philistine, Achish, king of Gath (1 Samuel 27 & 28).
- The incident at Ziklag, when the Amalekites took captive the wives and children of David and his men. David's own men talked of stoning him (1 Samuel 30).

David passed every test. He survived Saul's manhunts. He kept his passion for God. He overcame the temptation to take matters into his own hands. He kept his "band of brothers" united through all the predicaments they faced. He stayed true to his calling.

On the other side of the mountains of testing, David was rewarded with the kingdom. His benefits as king were undoubtedly extensive; however, I consider David's kingship-preparation, through the tests he faced, of equal or greater value.

> Many of our tests form a training ground for future accomplishment.

Throughout the years of adversity and trial, David received the character development and leadership training that distinguished him during his illustrious forty-year reign. David led the people of Israel with "skillful hands" and "integrity of heart" (Psalm 78:72), qualities that were honed during his long and harsh testing process.

Many of our tests form a training ground for future accomplishment. Even in cases when we may fail tests, the preparation for and from such tests will prove to be valuable in the future. None of the efforts we put forth ever go to waste.

I encourage you to prepare as diligently as possible for foreseeable tests; then, once the tests begin, ask God to maximize the potential each test has of building you up from the inside out. Regardless of the outcome of the test, you will be better for it — guaranteed!

CHAPTER 5

POP QUIZ!

Pop Quiz!

~ The true test of character is not how much we know how to do, but how we behave when we don't know what to do. ~

John W. Holt Jr.

During my time in school, I can hardly remember any examination process that was enjoyable for me. Test preparation was grueling and the actual tests were intense. Pop quizzes were the most stressful.

A pop quiz is essentially an examination administered without prior warning. Unexpected tests are especially challenging due to the element of surprise.

From time to time, I have dreams involving familiar classroom settings from my high school or college days. The teacher or professor walks in, stands by his/her desk and announces, "Please put away all books and notebooks. It is time for a quiz." I am always relieved when I wake up from those dreams and realize all I have to do is go to work—no quiz!

The key difference between a pop quiz and a standard exam is preparation. In the case of announced tests, students have advance notice; with pop quizzes, they don't. In order to do well on quizzes, students must prepare for a test that

The Next Test

may or may not come. In other words, pop quizzes demand a continual state of test-readiness.

Although life's challenges generally outdo those posed by academic exams, the principle applies: Tests often commence without warning or precedent, allowing no time for additional preparation.

On a few occasions, miscommunication or a particular move of the Spirit put me in situations where I had to speak at an event without prior notice. I'll never forget arriving a few minutes late at a packed out service, where I was apprehended in the parking lot by the Master of Ceremonies. "We're all waiting for you!" he exclaimed. There I was, hoping I'd find an open seat in the back somewhere, when, unbeknownst to me, I was listed on the program as the first preacher for the event!

Someone had forgotten to notify me. I did not have notes. I had neither prayed nor fasted to prepare my heart for ministry. Within minutes, I was on the platform looking at a large crowd that expected me to say something meaningful. That was an unannounced test of the highest order for me. To pass it, I had to rely upon two factors: 1. My identity as a child of God. 2. The deposits God had already made in my life. Both significantly influence our performance on life's pop quizzes.

Pop Quiz!

As a father, I would never give my children an assignment that represents me and my household, without properly equipping or supporting them to carry it out. How much more would God ensure His children have His backing through all unexpected tests and trials! God created us. We belong to Him. We are called by His Name. We constitute His Kingdom. He will never leave us, nor forsake us. We are children of the "most High God!"

I am always intrigued by survival stories. Men, women or children get trapped or buried under rubble for days after natural disasters. Travelers get stranded in the wilderness during blizzards. Climbers lose their way on a mountain. Airplane crash survivors end up in a jungle.

> As much as test-performance can be enhanced by preparation, each of us has remarkable deposits within us to excel when circumstances put us on the spot.

Despite circumstances which push bodies, minds and souls beyond conceivable limits, people manage to come out alive. In interviews following their rescues, victims often attribute their survival to reserves of endurance and resolve, of which they were not aware.

God has equipped us spiritually, mentally and physically with extraordinary capacity for perseverance and overcoming, especially when our lives are consecrated to Him. As much as test-performance can be enhanced by preparation, each of us has remarkable deposits within us to excel when circumstances put us on the spot.

~

Unlike the unexpected tests mentioned above, which can threaten our existence, some pop quizzes have the potential to launch us into great levels of significance. King Solomon was established in fame and fortune through two events: One was supernatural; the other temporal. In both cases, Solomon was tested with questions for which he had no preparation. The two events were pop quizzes.

The first test came during Solomon's first encounter with God:

> *At Gibeon the LORD appeared to Solomon in a dream by night; and God said, "Ask! What shall I give you?"*
> 1 Kings 3:5

This was a huge moment for Solomon. The Almighty God Himself appeared to the king of Israel with a "blank check." From the way He asked the question, it appears God was willing to grant Solomon whatever he asked. It wasn't a trick question, yet God was testing Solomon's heart.

The king did not have an opportunity to study the matter or weigh his options. He could not take the time to build relationship with the Lord and

Pop Quiz!

learn more about His ways, to ensure a proper response. Solomon had to answer out of the abundance of his heart right then and there.

His response was remarkable:

> *Now, O LORD my God, You have made Your servant king instead of my father David, but I am a little child; I do not know how to go out or come in...Therefore give to Your servant an understanding heart to judge Your people, that I may discern between good and evil. 1 Kings 3:7, 9*

God was pleased with Solomon's request:

> *Then God said to him: "Because you have asked this thing, and have not asked long life for yourself, nor have asked riches for yourself, nor have asked the life of your enemies, but have asked for yourself understanding to discern justice, behold, I have done according to your words; see, I have given you a wise and understanding heart...and I have also given you what you have not asked: both riches and honor, so that there shall not be anyone like you among the kings all your days. 1 Kings 3:11-13*

Solomon aced the pop quiz. His response to God's question was not a lucky guess. The preparation for that particular quiz, and the

The Next Test

character deposit from which Solomon drew the right answer, began long before Solomon became king:

> *When I was my father's son, tender and the only one in the sight of my mother, He also taught me, and said to me: "Get wisdom! Get understanding! Wisdom is the principal thing; therefore get wisdom. And in all your getting, get understanding."* Proverbs 4:3-7

The second pop quiz, which was catalytic in establishing Solomon, took place after the completion of the construction of the temple and his palace. The queen of Sheba paid Solomon a visit. Her purpose for making the trip to Jerusalem was to put Solomon's wisdom to the test:

> *Now when the queen of Sheba heard of the fame of Solomon concerning the name of the LORD, she came to test him with hard questions. She came to Jerusalem with a very great retinue, with camels that bore spices, very much gold, and precious stones; and when she came to Solomon, she spoke with him about all that was in her heart.* 1 Kings 10:1-2

Solomon received the queen well. He extended splendid hospitality, and met all her expectations.

Pop Quiz!

> *So Solomon answered all her questions; there was nothing so difficult for the king that he could not explain it to her.*
> 1 Kings 10:3

Solomon had no way of knowing or preparing for the queen's questions ahead of time; neither did he know exactly what it would take to touch her heart. He approached this high-level state visit with what his upbringing and his God-encounters had established within his mind, heart and spirit.

The queen of Sheba was overwhelmed by what she experienced during her visit. The splendor of Solomon's kingdom, and especially the king's wisdom, opened up the queen's heart to God. It also opened her purse:

> "Blessed be the LORD your God, who delighted in you, setting you on the throne of Israel! Because the LORD has loved Israel forever, therefore He made you king, to do justice and righteousness." Then she gave the king one hundred and twenty talents of gold, spices in great quantity, and precious stones. There never again came such abundance of spices as the queen of Sheba gave to King Solomon.
> 1 Kings 10:9-10

Solomon's upbringing and readiness enabled him to fare well on both pop quizzes—one from God; the other from the queen—thus launching

Solomon to the pinnacle of his reign, and Israel to great heights of prosperity and influence.

~

In the remainder of this chapter, I present a particular pop quiz I face often within the spiritual environment in which I operate and help facilitate as a leader.

Many things happen in the course of church services, prayer meetings, healing services and conferences, which at least initially, I can neither understand, nor explain. Whether it is "outside of the box" revelatory teachings, extraordinary miracles, strange signs and wonders, dramatic deliverances, demonic manifestations, or people acting purely out of strong emotion, sometimes I feel uncomfortable in church.

I am not challenged as much by signs or manifestations, because I have a passion for the supernatural. My test as a leader is to discern accurately the spiritual atmosphere so I can respond quickly and decisively in a way that honors God's ways and encourages people to continue to pursue Him.

The way we respond to the moving of the Holy Spirit is critical. If we get the right sense of what He is doing, and allow Him to lead us, we will maximize the impact of the spiritual momentum the Spirit creates. I have witnessed some extraordinary physical healings and life-transforming encounters come forth out of such moments. On the other hand, if we wrongly deem people's responses to God as carnal or demonic manifestations, we may exercise our authority inappropriately, shut people down, grieve the Holy Spirit and miss the Lord's will for a meeting or an entire season.

Within God's government lies a beautiful, yet delicate balance between freedom to worship, proper order, Spirit flow, the operation of spiritual gifts, adherence to protocol, respect, honor and decency; all within a context of faith, trust and unconditional love.

At our church, we have established many protocols to help us discern and direct the flow of the Spirit. We have developed systems of communication among our staff, ushers, members of prayer teams, etc. Our policies and core values are posted in our weekly bulletins and on framed posters on the wall. We evaluate situations on a weekly basis during staff meetings, and make necessary adjustments. As much as we try to prepare for different scenarios, and as much experience as we may have gained over the years, we frequently encounter unprecedented and unexpected tests.

While praying through some of the dilemmas posed by such moments, I came up with three words: *integrity*, *fruit* and *grace*. The three words grew into two questions and one declaration:

1. Does this person have *integrity*? In other words, has he/she earned credibility in the house through sound relationships and a good track record?
2. Is there *fruit* in the person's life? Jesus assured us we "will know them by their fruit." "Thornbushes" don't produce grapes. Figs don't come from "thistles" (Matthew 7:16).
3. God's *grace* will always cover any honest mistakes someone makes, as long as the other two questions can be answered affirmatively. His "grace is sufficient for [us], for His strength is made perfect in weakness" (2 Corinthians 12:9).

We consider these two questions and one declaration whenever someone is "given the microphone", when there are public manifestations which are out of the ordinary, or when we find ourselves in "uncharted" spiritual waters. Fear and suspicion have no room to land. The possibility of missing God is minimized.

At times when we are quizzed as such, we have great confidence God will extend His wonderful grace over everything we cannot address out of our established protocols or pull up from the God-deposits in our lives. He is always faithful; and He honors those who honor Him.

I encourage you not to fear the quizzes that pop when the Spirit moves. He who "has begun a

Pop Quiz!

good work in you will complete it until the day of Jesus Christ" (Philippians 1:6).

> *....for it is God who works in you both to will and to do for His good pleasure.*
> Philippians 2:13

CHAPTER 6

TEST CHEATS

Test Cheats

~ Why is there so much controversy about drug testing? I know plenty of guys who would be willing to test any drug they could come up with! ~

George Carlin

~ In God's Kingdom, certificates and diplomas have no value unless they are earned. ~

I always chuckle when I remember a specific episode that occurred during my first day on the job at a Christian school, where I had been hired as a teacher.

I was addressing a group of fifth, sixth, and seventh graders. The counsel I had received from well-meaning friends was to make sure I came across ultra-strict and ruthlessly uncompromising on the first day; then loosen up a bit as time went on. As much as I wanted to love on the kids, declare we would have a great year together, and build relationship with them, I went with the lean-and-mean advice. I read my class "the riot act."

"And when it comes to cheating, let me warn you there is no trick in the book I have not already tried; so don't even think about it."

The students sat on the edge of their seats. Ears were perked, and their body language invited me to *elaborate*. I bit the hook! I continued, drawing from a mental list of cheating techniques I had

The Next Test

(unfortunately) learned and used for tests in my BC (Before Christ) school days.

"I know about writing notes on your hand...using peripheral vision to get answers from your neighbors...about little cheat-sheets tied with strings and taped up your forearm for quick retraction...and as for writing answers on toilet paper, replacing the rolls in the bathrooms before the test, and then asking permission to use the bathroom so you can get answers from your toilet paper rolls, forget about it! I will..."

The semi-coherent mumbling of a fifth-grader interrupted me mid-sentence:

"Mmm, that's a good one. Never thought of the toilet paper one before – thanks!"

I glared right at him, demanding, "What did you just say?" Without missing a beat, he repeated his remark. The class studied my face intensely, waiting for a response. Out of the corner of my mouth, the first sign of a smirk emerged. It turned into a smile; then I laughed, and so did my students. So much for being Mr. Tough Guy out of the gate! The rest of our day was pleasant and productive; so was the rest of the year.

My initial approach lacked authority and credibility, because I was actually cheating myself and the class by posing to be someone other than who I really was. When I loosened up, my phony façade shattered, making room for an atmosphere of honesty, freedom and honor to start developing.

Test Cheats

Over the next few weeks and months, my students and I formed a relationship characterized by sincerity and mutual respect. Together, we established a classroom culture, in which cheating was both unnecessary and unthinkable. In eleven years of teaching, I dealt with students cheating on tests or assignments only a handful of times.

The objective of this chapter is not to belabor the obvious facts that cheating is wrong, that cheaters are in error, and the consequences for such actions can be severe. Rather, the chapter aims to highlight the benefits of establishing and operating within an environment similar to the one we enjoyed in my classroom.

~

I define cheating as working toward favorable results by illegitimate means. In an academic setting, for example, students may seek test answers from neighbors or their smart phones. They may plagiarize in their term papers. They may utilize inappropriate study aids to avoid required readings. All cheating techniques are illegitimate means by which students try to obtain favorable results—passing grades, academic credits, diplomas, degrees, etc.

Cheating looks different in other realms of life; however, the same definition applies. People cheat on their taxes for more

> Process and price are two important common denominators associated with most worthwhile accomplishments in life.

take-home pay. Spouses are unfaithful to their partners in pursuit of more harmonious relationships. Athletes use illegal steroids to win games, meets or championships. Unethical business leaders scam investors or consumers to make a "quick buck." In each case, "cheaters" pursue favorable results by illegitimate means.

Process and price are two important common denominators associated with most worthwhile accomplishments in life. Good things, or *favorable results*, come through process, and exact a price. All forms of cheating stem from the unwillingness to submit to process and pay a price.

Consider our church's expansion project mentioned in the *Introduction*. The construction of the new building involved an intense four-month process, comprised of carefully planned and well-coordinated functions by a large number of professionals. Among them were site developers, landscapers, pavers, concrete contractors, framers, roofers, carpenters, sheet-rockers, insulators, tapers, electricians, plumbers, sound and light specialists, water sprinkler installers and painters.

Before any of these folks could begin work, the church had to obtain a building permit from the town. The entire permit-seeking process lasted ten months. I personally attended many meetings with town consultants, and about a dozen official meetings with town officers and committees.

Test Cheats

At each meeting, I presented site plans and blueprints, which had been drawn up by our engineers, architects, surveyors and landscapers. The process of producing plans began one year prior to our application for the permit.

In terms of monetary expense, the project required tens of thousands of dollars before groundbreaking and hundreds of thousands, overall. Tag onto "the price" the huge investment of time by our volunteers and the significant disruption of church activities during construction.

The wonderful building we are now enjoying is the favorable result of an expensive and multi-faceted two-year process. During that time, our church family was tested in many ways. Personally, as I stated earlier, the project cost me dearly. As rigorous as the tests may have been, circumventing the process and skimping on the price was never an option.

Not only did we want to honor God and His ways, we viewed that particular project as only one of numerous expansion endeavors within the scope of our long-term vision and calling. A precedent of cheating would catch up to us in the near or distant future.

> People cheat when the temptation to cheat successfully exploits their character flaws.

The Next Test

Placing our immediate challenges against the backdrop of the "bigger picture" helps us develop and maintain the right attitude during times of testing.

~

The mindsets and personal disciplines which keep people from cheating do not emanate from the threat of punishment; rather, from strength of character. People cheat when the temptation to cheat successfully exploits their character flaws. There is always opportunity to cheat; whether we do so or not depends on our internal moral, ethical and spiritual makeup.

People who place a high value on integrity and honor will not trade such virtues for the cheap, short-term relief offered by dishonesty.

Amazingly, on the very day I started writing this portion of the chapter, I faced the following testing scenario:

Danielle and I borrowed a moving truck from a local storage company to transport donated furniture. When we went to sign for the truck, the manager said the gas needle was on "Full", and to please return it that way. Knowing we were not planning to drive far, she also implied we would not need to add gasoline as long as the needle remained on "Full". We responded with, "We will be happy to top off the tank with gas."

The assignment went so smoothly, we ended up traveling less than expected. We drove three miles each way from the storage unit to our destination, a total of six miles. The gas needle did not move from the "Full" position in the slightest. Although we were still in compliance with the manager's request to return the truck on "Full", we had committed to top off the tank.

In the Kingdom of God, a promise is binding. Unless we are released from our commitment by those involved in the agreement, we must honor our word at all cost:

> *God, who gets invited to dinner at your place? How do we get on your guest list? "Walk straight, act right, tell the truth...Keep your word even when it costs you.* Psalm 15:1-2, 5 (The Message)

The company manager would have been satisfied without the top-off, for the gas needle was on "Full". *God* would only be satisfied with one hundred percent integrity on our part. Our desire to please *Him* far outweighed any seemingly unnecessary inconvenience or expense. We drove across town to a gas station, waited in line for an open bay, went inside to pre-pay, pumped the gas, and then walked back inside for change—yes, we had overpaid with a five dollar bill! Our cost was minimal; the negative impact of violating our word could have been enormous.

The Next Test

> What propels us to do right is not the doom of wrongdoing, but the potential benefits of doing right.

The corruption of values and standards may be very subtle at first, but it delivers devastating blows in the long run. Compromised ethics and morals are always at the root of marital infidelity, exploitation, fraud, tax evasion, copyright infringement, steroid use, plagiarism and every other form of cheating. All transgressions begin small and grow with time. Being completely truthful and honoring at all times is the best way to avoid the heartache and dysfunction associated with such offenses.

~

Our commitment to honesty and truth must not be generated by fear of the painful consequences for cheating. Instead, it must originate from our understanding of the benefits of walking with integrity. What propels us to do right is not the doom of wrongdoing, but the potential benefits of doing right.

Beyond respect and honor through relationship with their teacher, I believe my students did not cheat in class because of a system of learning (and testing) in which cheating was unnecessary.

Each class had a small number of students, hence opportunities for one-on-one instruction. Regularly-checked homework assignments, test reviews and progress reports enabled teachers to assess students' progress before tests or graded assignments. Moreover, students could retake tests or request extra-credit projects to improve their grades. In short, we gave the kids every chance to succeed, while eliminating the fear of failure from the equation.

Our Heavenly Father has done the same. Instead of the bondage to fear, He gave us "love, power, and a sound mind". The first chapter of 2 Peter says God, by "His divine power has given to us all things that pertain to life and godliness." We access His marvelous blessings by knowing "Him who called us by glory and virtue." Peter also affirms that God has given to us "Exceedingly great and precious promises", by which we become "partakers of the divine nature, having escaped the corruption that is in the world through lust" (2 Peter 1:4).

Wow! God doesn't just give us what we need to pass the tests of life; He makes us more like Him in the process, promoting us from "faith unto faith" and "glory to glory."

~

During the first twenty years of my life, I did not have a relationship with God. As it pertains to His laws and commandments and the principles by which His Kingdom is governed, I was an outright "cheater". I lived for myself and tried to get ahead by doing things my way. I often disregarded or

The Next Test

circumvented both the price and process necessary for working through prescribed tests.

The biblical term for my condition would be "sinner." There is no way to sugarcoat this—I lived in sin without giving any consideration to the person and nature of God or His ways.

The fear of judgment and punishment for my sins did not draw me to God; neither did hard-hitting preaching about eternal suffering in hell. What changed me was God's unconditional love. He embraced me, forgave me, and gave me favor. God showed me the way to His heart. He has been drawing me deeper into the realms of His love ever since.

I share my story in the context of this chapter on cheating, because I believe someone who can relate may be reading this book at this very moment. You may recognize your sin and wrongdoing in various areas of your life. You may have made some wrong choices. You may have associated with unscrupulous people. You may have been unfaithful to your spouse. You may have been dishonest in the handling of financial matters. You may have chosen the easy way out, in an attempt to circumvent the process. If so, God is ready to extend His grace to you at this very moment. I encourage you to pray a simple prayer, similar to the one I prayed in 1991, inviting Jesus to come into my life:

Test Cheats

Father, I thank You for Your love and mercy. I recognize Your hand is on my life right now.

I admit I have not honored You. I have not followed Your ways. I confess my sins. I ask You to forgive me. I invite Jesus into my heart as Savior and Lord.

Thank You, Jesus, for paying the price for my sins. I submit to Your process. I commit to live the rest of my days for You. Thank You for making a way for me to obtain favorable results by legitimate means! Bless me, lead me and keep me, I pray.

In Jesus' Name, Amen!

If you just prayed that prayer, I congratulate you for your new or restored relationship with God. I am certain He will order and direct your steps. May the Lord's grace and love continually be made known to you, and may He guide and help you through every test.

Jesus truly is wonderful!

> *Then they willingly received Him into the boat, and immediately the boat was at the land where they were going.*
> John 6:21

The Next Test

CHAPTER 7

THE TEST OF SUCCESS

The Test of Success

~ Testing leads to failure, and failure leads to understanding. ~

Burt Rutan

~ Nearly all men can stand adversity, but if you want to test a man's character, give him power. ~

Abraham Lincoln

A few years ago, I realized unnecessary conflict was a part of my life. My prayer life was periodically preoccupied with spiritual battles which were identical with previous confrontations. It was a vicious cycle:

I would come under attack. I would cry out to God for help. God would come through for me and give me victory. I would walk in peace for a while. Then, I would come under attack again.

The circumstances were different each time, but the disheartening fact was unchanged: I had battled against the same oppressive mindsets, emotions or demonic entities before, and by God's grace I had overcome. Why was I up against those same forces?

As a human being, living in a fallen world, I expected trouble to manifest from time to time. I did not expect having to face the same trouble repeatedly. Losing ground which had been gained by fighting "the good fight" earlier made absolutely no sense to me. I became determined to find why I was frequently embroiled in unnecessary conflict.

The conclusions from a series of "internal audits" indicated familiar issues had been resurfacing because I had been letting down my guard shortly after winning victories. The root cause of my inconsistencies was complacency and pride.

I would pray, meditate on the Scriptures and worship extensively during times of testing, but would cut back on my devotional times once I obtained the breakthrough. I learned how to position myself before God and man in order to prevail, but then lost my spiritual edge during times of peace and rest. On a spiritual level, I did much better handling hardship or persecution than I did success and promotion.

When we do well in an area of our lives, a sinister voice from the realm of darkness begins to vie for our attention. The enemy tries to flatter us for our accomplishments, without giving proper recognition and praise to the Lord, who makes any success possible. If we fall for that trick and think more highly of ourselves than we should, we will move farther and farther away from God's empowering and sustaining grace that got us there in the first place.

To overcome this particular challenge, I resorted to a force instilled in me through my Special Forces training—intense discipline.

Within a day or so after glorious meetings in which God mightily demonstrates His power; the completion of large projects; the fulfillment of significant aspirations; favorable public recognition; extravagant material blessing; or the reaching of any other success-markers in my life, I enter a self-imposed heart-alignment and attitude-adjustment process. I recommend this or something similar to it for everyone interested in maintaining the right heart posture through times of victory and success:

- Celebrate every victory.
- Enjoy the elation and encouragement of the moment.
- Get alone with God and thank Him for His grace. Worship Jesus, even for a few moments.
- Direct any praise from people toward God (be genuine, avoiding false humility).
- Read John 15:1-8.
- Through mentors, role models, teachings or readings, maintain a focus on vision and life-purpose.
- Mentally insert the recent success story in the thick manuscript that represents our destiny.

Adhering to this particular regimen helps prevent battle repeats and success-related failures.

Lasting success requires consistent effort, resolute focus and an accurate perspective of where we stand with God. In John 15, Jesus presents a vivid picture regarding our connection with Him and the Father. We are the branches, Jesus is the vine, and the Father is the vinedresser (vs. 1).

Jesus clearly states we have been chosen as branches with the purpose of bearing lasting fruit:

> *You did not choose Me, but I chose you and appointed you that you should go and bear fruit, and that your fruit should remain...* John 15:16

The whole purpose for planting and tending a vineyard is to enjoy the fruit of the vine. Non-fruit-bearing branches are eliminated. The vinedresser only invests additional time, resources, and energy into branches which have proven to be productive.

> *Every branch in Me that does not bear fruit He takes away.* John 15:2

The Father grants the remaining branches the privilege of bearing fruit — the most glorious aspect of the vine's growth cycle. We, as the vine branches, can only produce grapes if we are connected to the vine, Jesus:

> *Abide in Me and I in you. As the branch cannot bear fruit of itself, unless it abides in the vine, neither can you, unless you abide in Me. I am the vine, you are the branches. He who abides in Me, and I in him bears much fruit; for without Me you can do nothing.* John 15:4-5

When we abide in Christ by keeping His commandments (vs. 10), we bear fruit that remains. Fruitfulness is success, and that is the purpose for which the branches are formed out of the vine.

What the vinedresser does next with the productive branches seems bewildering:

> *Every branch that bears fruit He prunes, that it may bear more fruit.* John 15:2

Think about it. All the praise and glory for the vine's productivity goes to the vinedresser (the Father), who plants and tends the vineyard. The vine (Jesus) is also praised for being fruitful. As for the branches (us), out of which the fruit actually came forth; they get pruned shortly after their grapes are harvested.

The vinedresser uses the sharp blades of pruning shears or clippers to cut off the very parts of the vine that have successfully brought forth fruit in the past! The branches which had grown so significantly by being properly connected to the vine are now reduced in size and fullness. This

The Next Test

may seem like harsh treatment of good, productive branches.

> Though harsh and seemingly punishing initially, tests and trials that follow "bountiful harvests" in our lives offer us the opportunity to grow further and ultimately bear more fruit.

Not only may the branches themselves appear to be wrongly penalized, so does the vine as a whole. Generally speaking, the pruning process places stress on the vine. With parts of branches or entire branches gone, the vine has fewer leaves for photosynthesis and other vital life-sustaining processes. Moreover, it does not look as full and vibrant as when its fruit-producing branches (now clipped back) were at their peak performance. Pruning is a test.

What initially may seem questionable practice on the vinedresser's part eventually proves to be the best and often the only way for further growth and fruitfulness. The pruning process which stressed and thus *tested* the vine, procures a larger, fuller vine abounding with fruit, even more than before the pruning!

You and I were created for the purpose of consistently producing large quantities of fruit; fruit that remains. Though harsh and seemingly punishing initially, tests and trials that follow "bountiful harvests" in our lives offer us the opportunity to grow further and ultimately bear more fruit.

The Test of Success

~

Another key for lasting success is recognizing the importance of "standing."

> *Finally, my brethren, be strong in the Lord and in the power of His might. Put on the whole armor of God, that you may be able to stand against the wiles of the devil. For we do not wrestle against flesh and blood, but against principalities, against powers, against the rulers of the darkness of this age, against spiritual hosts of wickedness in the heavenly places. Therefore take up the whole armor of God, that you may be able to withstand in the evil day, and having done all, to stand.*
> Ephesians 6:10-11, 13

This portion from Ephesians 6 is perhaps the most quoted in reference to spiritual warfare. For most of my life as a student of the Bible, whenever I read these verses, I envisioned battle scenes in the heavenly realms and intense confrontations with demonic forces.

In my mind's eyes, I saw Christian soldiers clad with God's armor fighting hard in the spirit realm against the forces of darkness. As a member of the Lord's army, I would take up the various components of the armor and symbolically take hold of them or put them on, often acting out the motions! The breastplate of righteousness, the helmet of salvation, the belt of truth, foot coverings of the preparation of the Gospel of peace, the shield of faith, and sword of the spirit. I would "put on" the whole armor and then pray intensely in the spirit. I was ready to fight hard against the enemy and prevail.

I rarely, if ever, won great victories that way; in fact, I experienced some severe spiritual beatings.

On one occasion, Danielle and I, while en route to Cyprus, spent a night in the city of Amsterdam. Our airline, which had made a mistake with our flights, put us up in a hotel two blocks from the city's red light district. Upon our realization of where we were and our failure to negotiate a different hotel, we entered our room and went right into "warfare prayer." I remember quoting Scriptures, putting on the armor, rebuking all the demons and serving all the prevailing evil principalities notice that we were in town and meant business.

After a short nap, we decided to take a walk. As much as we tried to avoid the red light district, we got lost and ended up smack dab in the center of it. I quickly discovered my warfare mentality and approach was ineffective in that particular battlefield. Instead of viewing the porn shop owners, drug dealers, prostitutes, and revelers with love and compassion, I judged them and became angry at them for polluting the streets through their "partnerships with the devil." I became agitated with beggars and street performers. I despised the cafes offering drugs on the menu. Before long, I resented the entire city and wanted out of there as soon as possible.

Back at the hotel, Danielle and I had a rough time. We heard shouting and screaming throughout the morning hours. We hardly slept. We argued about what to watch on TV. We were terrified someone might try to break in our room. Then someone *did* try to break in (Thankfully, we had propped a chair against the door earlier). By the time we left Amsterdam the next morning, we were miserable.

It was not God's will for us to spend a night in fear and leave the city angry and exasperated; and it was most certainly not God's will that we sin. We did as badly, if not worse, than everyone else in town, by judging people and speaking curses over the city.

I attribute my failure in the Amsterdam incident and other similar encounters to my misunderstanding and misapplication of the Scriptures pertaining to spiritual warfare. I became so preoccupied with the mental images I had conjured up of fighting and contending, that I overlooked the three mentions of the word,

> All success comes and lasts when we are in right standing with Jesus!

"stand" in Ephesians 6:10-13. The whole purpose for taking up the armor of God is so that when all is said and done we will be found *standing*.

I began to develop a different mental picture, one in which I was still in God's army, wearing His armor, but instead of swinging the sword and deflecting arrows with my spear, I was just standing. Standing in a state of rest and peace, instead of striving. Standing in recognition that Jesus won the war over sin and death, and we already have the victory. Standing in awe of God's glory and splendor, which trumps all evil.

Successful warring on life's battlefields stems from yielding to God, not fighting the devil. We take our best stand for God when we stand *by* Jesus in relationship. The battle is the Lord's, and it is won, "not by might, nor by power, but by My Spirit says the Lord of hosts" (Zechariah 4:6).

Life is replete with seasons of spiritual and natural conflict. Through His life, death and resurrection, Jesus made a way for us to win each battle and to avoid unnecessary repeats of confrontations! All success comes and lasts when we are in right standing with Him!

> *For though He was crucified in weakness, yet He lives by the power of God. For we also are weak in Him, but we shall live with Him by the power of God toward you. Examine yourselves as to whether you are in the faith. Test*

yourselves. Do you not know yourselves, that Jesus Christ is in you? — unless indeed you are disqualified. But I trust that you will know that we are not disqualified. 2 Corinthians 13:4-6

CHAPTER 8

RE-TAKES

~ The difference between school and life? In school, you're taught a lesson and then given a test. In life, you're given a test that teaches you a lesson. ~

Tom Bodette

~ Failing tests = delayed advancement; avoiding tests = no advancement! ~

I attended middle and high school at The American Academy in Larnaca, Cyprus. I graduated in 1988. My parents and two brothers are also graduates of "The Academy." My father was part of the American Academy faculty as teacher and vice principal for twenty-six years. He and my mother were involved with the school for over thirty-seven years of their lives.

Ever since American missionaries founded the school in 1908, the American Academy has been one of the most respected academic institutions on the island.

Walking through the campus, one gets a feel for the school's illustrious history and its students' remarkable accomplishments. The halls of the administration building are adorned with trophy cases filled with cups, shields, metals, plaques and other forms of recognition. Several buildings are named after founders, benefactors and long-serving former administrators. Many American

The Next Test

Academy graduates have risen to places of notoriety in various spheres of society.

The Academy is noted for its commitment to academic excellence and overall character-development. The following is an excerpt from the home page of the American Academy website:

> *We expect students to be hardworking and committed, and we demand high standards of behavior so that effective teaching and learning can take place.*

Students aspiring to attend must do well on an entrance exam. Only one out of three applicants is accepted. Once enrolled, new students are immediately confronted with high expectations. Instructors' rigorous course requirements, their families' considerable financial commitment by way of tutoring for the entrance exam and annual tuition, and the ever-present backdrop of the school's long tradition and renowned status, put a heavy demand on students to perform and behave well.

Such was my feeling when I entered the Academy in seventh grade. I vividly remember my first day of classes. Each teacher's introductions, course descriptions, admonitions, warnings and presentations boiled down to this:

> *Academy students must act appropriately at all times; and must do their best in all their studies!*

Re-Takes

Following a lengthy (and rather intimidating) talk about the school's strict code of conduct and the consequences for misbehaving, every teacher introduced the textbook(s) for his/her class, followed by specific protocols for the completion of homework assignments. We were then admonished to take extensive notes in class, and we were briefed on written assignments, quizzes, tests, finals, grading scales and report cards.

By the end of the day, after five similar pitches, I was overwhelmed. While trying to sort through huge mountains of expectation and responsibility, I found hope in one piece of information. It was barely mentioned, and not even by every teacher; however, on the evening of my first day at the Academy, it was my "emotional lifeline":

In the event someone failed a course, he/she could take a "re-exam" before the start of the next year.

I don't know if that policy encouraged other students, for none of us dared admit we were giving any consideration to failure. It encouraged me greatly. After all that talk of what I had to do and what I had live up to, it felt so good to know that somewhere in the workings of this venerated academic institution, which put such high value on success, provision had also been made for failure.

Though it was never discussed openly, I believe the re-exam concept brought relief to many

The Next Test

of my classmates, especially those who ended up needing re-exams.

There is a hope for second chances in all of us, because everyone recognizes that during the course of life, we all fail at something. Somewhere along the journey, each of us needs a re-take for a failed test.

> One of the most astounding facets of God's grace is that He entrusts us with the governance and administration of His kingdom in spite of His foreknowledge of our failures.

The gospel of salvation magnificently makes provision for failure, once and for all. Jesus paid for our sins and facilitated endless re-take opportunities for humanity through His sacrifice on the cross. Once we commit our lives to Him, none of our failures can ever be conclusive. Every mistake, omission, or act of willful disobedience gets covered by the manifold grace of God, when we repent. Then, we have a chance for a do-over.

Ephesians 2 says God, "who is rich in mercy," saved us by His grace, gave us life in Christ, "raised us up together," and seated us with Jesus "in the Heavenly places" (Ephesians 2:4-6) God's reason in doing so:

> *That in the ages to come, He might show the exceeding riches of His grace in His kindness toward us in Christ Jesus.* Ephesians 2:7.

One of the most astounding facets of God's grace is that He entrusts us with the governance and administration of His kingdom in spite of His foreknowledge of our failures.

For any followers of Christ who may often feel inadequate or unqualified to serve Him because of their shortcomings, I recommend Scripture passages featuring Jesus' disciples. Talk about people who needed re-takes! One chapter in particular, Luke 9, should be prescribed reading for all of us, especially new believers.

Consider the following areas, recorded in just one chapter, where the disciples did not quite make the grade:

- The twelve came to Jesus in unison after a powerful day of ministry, to convince Him to send the multitudes away because of the lateness of the hour and the lack of provision at that location. According to John's record, Jesus asked Philip, "Where shall we buy bread that these may eat? But this He said *to test him* (emphasis mine), for He, Himself knew what He would do." (John 6:5, 6). Philip's response, as well as that of the rest of the disciples—"We have no more than five loaves and two fish" (Luke 9:13) - clearly proves, they failed that

The Next Test

test. Even after all the miracles they had witnessed, Jesus' twelve disciples were still processing impossibilities naturally, instead of supernaturally. They looked at the crowd, considered their provisions and determined, "This is impossible."

- Peter misunderstands the purpose for the transfiguration and immediately responds to the encounter by suggesting they build three tabernacles on top of the mountain (Luke 9:33). (This incident constitutes our best evidence yet, that Peter had never been through a building program!)

- To the chagrin of a demon-possessed boy's father, the nine disciples who remained at the foot of the mountain--while Jesus, Peter, James, and John were encountering the Transfiguration--were unable to cast the demon out:

"I implored Your disciples to cast it out, but they could not." Luke 9:40

- Shortly after Jesus rebuked the demon, healed the child, and noted prayer and fasting as the catalyst for that type of breakthrough (indicating the lack thereof in the disciples), the twelve continued their strikeouts with a *"dispute"* as to *"which of them would be greatest."* (Luke 9:46)

- Next, came John's reporting of the disciples shutting down someone who was actually doing Kingdom work:

Now John answered and said, "Master, we saw someone casting out demons in Your name, and we forbade him because he does not follow with us." Luke 9:49

- Last but not least, James and John's response to the poor reception a Samaritan village gave Jesus' messengers, who went ahead of the Lord to "prepare for Him":

"Lord, do you want us to command fire to come down from Heaven and consume them, just as Elijah did?" John 9:54

The narratives immediately preceding and following the list of disciple-blunders recorded in Luke 9 are fascinating:

Then He called His twelve disciples together and gave them power and authority over all demons, and to cure diseases. Luke 9:1

Jesus entrusted the disciples with power and authority, although He was perfectly aware of their shortcomings, flawed mindsets and spiritual immaturity. Now, let us see what Jesus did *after* all the above-mentioned mistakes had been made:

> *After these things the Lord appointed seventy others also, and sent them two by two before His face into every city and place where He Himself was about to go.*
> Luke 10:1

Most ministerial leaders I know would have begun wondering if they chose the right people for the job, and rightly so; I would have had the same concerns. Jesus not only continued to give assignments to the twelve, He recruited into His service seventy more people like them!

~

One of the most important factors in every relationship, particularly the bond between mentor and protégé, is loyalty. I emphasize loyalty at the outset of every mentoring relationship I begin. Transparency and vulnerability foster an environment in which the benefits from impartation and life-sharing can be maximized for those involved in the relationship. Therefore, I don't "wear armor" around those to whom I open my heart.

One of my favorite Scriptures pertaining to loyalty is found in 1 Chronicles, chapter 12. Men from the tribes of Benjamin and Judah came to David at the stronghold he had established while being persecuted by King Saul. David met with them and spoke very clearly regarding loyalty:

> *If you have come peaceably to me to help me, my heart will be united with you; but if to betray me to my enemies, since there is no wrong in my hands, may the God of our fathers look and bring judgment.* 1 Chronicles 12:17

The response of the men reflected the attitude of their hearts:

> *"We are yours, O David;*
> *We are on your side, O son of Jesse!*
> *Peace, peace to you,*
> *And peace to your helpers!*
> *For your God helps you."*
> 1 Chronicles 12:18

The men of Benjamin and Judah would be loyal to David. I am committed to maintain the same heart attitude with every mentor to whom I submit myself, and I expect nothing less from every man with whom I share my life. Both as a mentor and protégé, I consider loyalty one of the most significant elements in any discipleship relationship.

By the time Jesus was crucified, every disciple had failed the test of loyalty. Simon Peter failed most miserably.

The Next Test

During one of His intimate times with the disciples before His arrest, Jesus predicted an "examination" all disciples would "flunk":

> *Then Jesus said to them, "All of you will be made to stumble because of Me this night, for it is written:*
> *' I will strike the Shepherd,*
> *And the sheep will be scattered.'*
> Mark 14:27

None of the disciples received Jesus' words. Peter was the first to claim he would stand by his Lord, even if he had to stand alone:

> *"Even if all are made to stumble, yet I will not be."* Mark 14:29

Peter made the mistake of underestimating the test, while overestimating his own ability. He went so far as to claim he could perform better than everyone else.

We must approach all our trials in life with humility and courage. Humility enables us to obtain an accurate assessment of each challenge. Courage comes from God when we wholeheartedly trust Him to help us through. In that particular instance, Peter lacked the appropriate humility and courage. Unfortunately, he was also unaware of his deficiencies.

Jesus made His prophesy about Peter even more specific:

> *"Today, even this night, before the rooster crows twice, you will deny Me three times."* Mark 14:30

Peter responded by being even more emphatic about his ability to pass the test of loyalty. The other disciples followed suit:

> *"If I have to die with You, I will not deny You!" And they all said likewise.* Mark 14:31

Within hours, the fear of man prevailed over all the disciples' courage, and it put their good intentions to shame. Soldiers appeared, Judas betrayed Christ with a kiss, the Lord was arrested, and "they all forsook Him and fled." One of the disciples even ran naked after leaving his cloak with the soldiers who had tried to seize him (vs. 52).

Peter's denial of Jesus followed shortly thereafter, exactly as the Lord had predicted, down to the very last detail:

> *A second time the rooster crowed. Then Peter called to mind the word that Jesus had said to him, "Before the rooster crows twice, you will deny Me three times." And when he thought about it, he wept.* Mark 14:72

The Next Test

The most inspiring factor in the story of Peter's denial is found in a short interchange between Jesus and Peter before the Lord was arrested:

> *And the Lord said, "Simon, Simon! Indeed, satan has asked for you, that he may sift you as wheat. But I have prayed for you, that your faith should not fail; and when you have returned to Me, strengthen your brethren."*
> Luke 22:31-32

> Before Peter ever faced the test he would fail, Jesus made provision for a re-take.

Jesus foresaw Peter's disloyalty; therefore, He interceded for the disciple. The Lord then foretold Peter's loyalty failure, saying, "After you have returned to Me, strengthen your brethren." One only returns to what he/she leaves or separates from. Jesus predicted a separation between Peter and Himself. The *re-take* element is found in the last three words of verse 32—"…strengthen your brethren."

Before Peter ever faced the test he would fail, Jesus made provision for a re-take. He declared Peter would be restored in relationship, and would carry out a significant post-restoration leadership assignment.

I particularly like The Message Bible rendition of the same verse:

"Simon, stay on your toes. Satan has tried his best to separate all of you from me, like chaff from wheat. Simon, I've prayed for you in particular that you not give in or give out. When you have come through the time of testing, turn to your companions and give them a fresh start."

God is not intimidated by our failures and shortcomings; and neither does He let them hinder His will and purpose for our lives. The post-ascension character qualities and ministry effectiveness of the disciples, especially Peter, recorded in the book of Acts, are in large part, the product of divinely orchestrated do-overs for failed tests.

Do you struggle with failure? Do you feel unworthy of God's love and trust when you make mistakes? Does shame or guilt attempt an entry or re-entry into your life following moments of deficiency or defeat? Be encouraged—Jesus Christ extends to you the same grace He extended to His disciples.

> Your failures and mine cannot hinder our destiny. Before we ever failed our first test, Jesus made a way for us to graduate with honors.

Through Jesus' sacrifice on the cross and the power of the Spirit "which raised Christ from the dead" (Romans 8:11), forgiveness and restoration are immediately attainable. Once we recognize our mistakes and repent, the Lord causes dark clouds

The Next Test

of shame, condemnation and unworthiness to dissipate. By the Holy Spirit, Jesus reconciles us to the Father; then, He immediately redeploys us into glorious realms of service and life.

Your failures and mine cannot hinder our destiny. Before we ever failed our first test, Jesus made a way for us to graduate with honors.

Thank God for re-takes!

Chapter 9

Study Mates

Study Mates

~ My best friend is the one who brings out the best in me. ~

Henry Ford

~ True friendship is a plant of slow growth, and must undergo and withstand the shocks of adversity before it is entitled to the appellation. ~

George Washington

During my junior and senior years in college and two years in graduate school, I prepared for tests and final exams by studying with small groups of fellow history majors.

We began our study sessions, which almost always featured caffeinated drinks, pizza and candy, at least a week before each test. We generally met in one of the classrooms on campus.

First, we shared our written notes from class, filling in gaps along the way. Then we collaborated in establishing study sheets with the important names and facts. We took turns narrating historical events and quizzed each other extensively, especially the night before the exam. We took bathroom breaks, stretch breaks and food breaks. Sometimes we studied for two or three hours; most times, we worked through the night.

Our study sessions were productive and fun. We talked and laughed a lot. During breaks, we shared personal anecdotes and life experiences. We encouraged each other and helped lighten the load of test-preparation. By the end of each meeting, our confidence levels soared. Everyone knew he/she could not have studied as effectively and as enjoyably on his/her own.

Once tests were returned, we celebrated with those who rejoiced over their results, and we comforted those who were disappointed. We developed strong bonds among us. I do not believe I would have survived some of my college and graduate courses without my study mates. I am very grateful for these friends.

Friends are gifts from God; study mates in the course of life. By definition, a friend is a person affectionately attached to another individual through feelings of personal regard. Building on that foundation of affection and personal regard, friends engage in conversation, share common interests, join in activities together, and become involved (sometimes deeply) in each other's lives. Friendships are especially precious during trials.

Everyone can recall seasons of testing, during which friends played a significant role by listening, comforting, encouraging and offering counsel. Friends help us through hardship.

What happens when friendship itself faces hardship? What dynamics are involved when "study mate" relationships get tested?

> Conflict is the testing ground on which the strength and depth of relationships are best assessed.

Time and/or distance apart, success, failure, suspicion, pride, envy, fear, betrayal and tragedy are some of the factors that often try friendships. All such challenges have the potential of festering into conflict. Conflict is the testing ground on which the strength and depth of relationships are best assessed.

The deepest and strongest relationship I have ever had is with my wife. At the time this book is being written, Danielle and I are celebrating fifteen years of marriage. We share life together on many different planes. We are husband and wife and the parents of three children. We co-labor in the establishing of our home and the raising of our sons and daughter. We are partners in domestic and marketplace ventures, involving financial resources. We are co-pastors of a church and serve alongside each other in various areas within the greater body of Christ.

At the core of our various roles and associations, Danielle and I are friends; best friends. Long before we joined hands at an altar, we were friends who worked together at a restaurant. Over time, we became friends who

The Next Test

shared input in each other's life. It was in that context I told Danielle she made a good move by breaking up with her boyfriend!

After Danielle gave her heart to the Lord, a very significant spiritual dimension was added to our friendship. We talked about the things of God and prayed together. Under the canopy of God's love, we shared life at a deeper level, increasingly opening our hearts to each other. We fell in love quickly. Soon we were engaged, making a pivotal shift toward marriage-preparation.

On our wedding day, Danielle and I merged our hearts and lives, forming a covenant relationship between two friends and God. A wonderful new realm opened up to us as lovers. Sexual intimacy is most fulfilling and enjoyable in the context of a strong friendship, within the covenant of marriage.

By divine assignment and appointment, Danielle and I always worked together. Shortly after our wedding, we taught at the same school and served as youth pastors. We spent countless hours talking, dreaming, laughing, pondering, maturing and growing together. Our friendship grew by leaps and bounds.

Within a few years, we started having children. Three kids within six years - we got busy! Our ministerial and family responsibilities continually increased; and so did our trials.

Following the birth of our daughter, we went through several difficult years. Most of our challenges were ministry-related. The tests got harder after we began to experience a powerful move of the Spirit in our church. For several years, we faced intense continual pressure from within and without.

Danielle and I fastened our seatbelts and tried to hold on. We prayed together a lot and trusted God to bring us through. We made time to talk, laugh and have fun together.

> Conflict influences our perception of the person with whom we take issue, especially when conflict is chronic.

By God's grace and our strong bonds of friendship, we held together through the shakings and beatings; however, over time, the conflict *around* us entered the confines of our relationship and became conflict *among* us.

The only way to preserve the core of our marriage--our friendship—was to strengthen it by growing in our understanding and application of biblical conflict resolution principles. Among the most significant keys God gave to us while our friendship and marriage were being tested, was fresh revelation regarding a virtue that carries tremendous conflict-resolving power: humility.

Conflict influences our perception of the person with whom we take issue, especially when conflict is chronic. Over time, the negative emotions evoked by disagreements and arguments can cause us to view our friends through conflict-shaded lenses. Once our perception of each other changes, the foundations of friendship start shaking.

For instance, a couple may struggle finding agreement in matters involving finances. The wife wants to save as much money as possible for home improvements and contingencies. He, on the other hand, feels they should save less and enjoy life more, as long as they stay within their means. Consequently, the wife turns down her husband's frequent suggestions for wardrobe additions, dining out and weekend getaways. Conversely, the husband frowns upon any mention of upgrading the plumbing and electrical in the apartment; nor does he want to hear about the furnace that is getting old and may need replacement.

If the couple continues to disagree and argue, eventually, the woman will begin to perceive her husband as a "spendthrift", while he considers his wife to be a "tightwad". Arguments will escalate each time the issues come up. Husband and wife will respond to each other based on perceptions that have developed through conflict, instead of the perceptions their friendship, romance and marriage were founded upon.

Danielle and I did not struggle with the issue above; however, we experienced this dynamic at work in other areas of our relationship. No matter how committed we were to working through things as they came up, and reconciling quickly, the problems kept recurring; and so did the possibility for erroneous perceptions.

Then we both came upon the following portion of Scripture:

> *Let nothing be done through selfish ambition or conceit, but in lowliness of mind let each esteem others better than himself. Let each of you look out not only for his own interests, but also for the interests of others.* Philippians 2:1-4

To begin with, it was encouraging to know we can look out for our own interests, just as long as we looked out for the interests of the other person as well. We also discovered that the practice of esteeming the other person better than ourselves eliminated every possibility of misperceiving our spouse. It was absolutely impossible for me to view my wife negatively—even during disagreements—when I consciously and sincerely chose to value her above myself.

Humility was the key. Once we humbled our hearts before God and each other, "self" gave way to "other". The revelation and application of this Scripture strengthened our marriage and helped us in all our relationships.

~

The Next Test

As much as we try to avoid controversial discussions, from time to time, we find ourselves in settings where fellow ministry leaders openly disagree with the doctrines and practices of our movement. One potential stumbling block, for example, is our position regarding the operation of the gifts of the Spirit in the Church.

Our belief happens to be that all nine gifts listed in 1 Corinthians 12 are available and functional in and through believers today. Some of our colleagues from other faith movements claim the gifts of the Holy Spirit ceased to operate in individuals after the passing of the last apostle. Any miraculous manifestations are ascribed to the sovereignty of God, not the working of God *through* His people.

Our disagreement on the matter presents the opportunity for faulty perceptions of each other to develop between our Christian co-laborers and us. If we bite that hook of division, and insist on "being right", we will view our brothers and sisters through the lenses of our doctrinal disagreements.

> Humility renders conflict incapable of festering into division and strife.

We do not have to be right. At our church, we have established core values of honor, respect and unconditional love toward all faith movements and their adherents. Regardless of where we stand on various issues, we perceive all Christian ministries as co-laborers, serving on the same side and for the same purpose of bringing glory to God.

By keeping a humble spirit, looking out for others' interests, and esteeming them above ourselves, we maintain a positive perception of them regardless of whether we agree with them or not. Thus, we are able to discuss matters and resolve issues between us without a bias from tainted perceptions. Humility renders conflict incapable of festering into division and strife.

I pray God will teach us humility so that we, as the body of Christ at large, can pass the test of unity, and then work together as "study mates" to prepare for the tests up ahead. May the following quotes about and directly from Jesus, the Word, take root in our hearts:

> *Let this mind be in you which was also in Christ Jesus, who, being in the form of God, did not consider it robbery to be equal with God, but made Himself of no reputation, taking the form of a bondservant, and coming in the likeness of men. And being found in appearance as a man, He humbled Himself and became obedient to the point of death, even the death of the cross.* Philippians 2:5-8

> *No longer do I call you servants, for a servant does not know what his master is*

The Next Test

doing; but I have called you friends, for all things that I heard from My Father I have made known to you. John 15:15

Chapter 10

Test Results

Test Results

> ~ *I've always believed that if you put in the work, the results will come.* ~
>
> Michael Jordan

I am not a big fan of gymnastics, figure skating or diving; however, I am always inspired by a feature all three events have in common. The score of each competing athlete is determined by a number of judges. Athletes perform and judges allocate points, which are either added together or averaged. The score athletes receive for each trial represents the collective evaluation of all judges present.

In each of these three events (and others judged similarly), there is a short lapse between the time a diver, skater or gymnast completes his/her attempt, and the posting of results.

Whenever such events are televised, cameras closely follow the athletes awaiting their scores, while the judges compile their totals. During those brief moments, body language and facial expressions communicate each athlete's personal evaluation rather well. In most cases, it is rather easy to predict scores accurately, just by watching the athletes' post-performance reaction.

I am most intrigued when the athletes awaiting their scores know they have competed exceptionally well. The gymnast sticks the landing after a sensational routine on the parallel bars, ending with a triple back-flip. The Olympic diver emerges from the depths of the pool to the flashes of cameras and the applause of the audience. She performed a difficult high-dive, involving several twists and somersaults and ending with a superb vertical entry. A figure-skater completes his sensational sequence of spins, turns, edge-changes and jumps, with a perfectly-executed triple axel.

The beaming face; the excited wave to the crowd; the bear hug for coach; the fist pump; the tears; the joy. Such elation for a stellar performance! Athletes then shift their focus to the scoreboards, their eyes full of hope and expectation.

The victorious result competitors, especially Olympians, eagerly anticipate during the few seconds before scores are announced, represents much more than a positive evaluation for their most-recent effort. It is a reward that justifies and honors years of labor and trial.

A childhood dream. Small beginnings. Years of training. Countless lessons. Exciting wins. Disappointing losses. Disheartening injuries. Strict diets. Demanding coaches. Extreme discipline. Ups and downs. Agony and ecstasy… So much work has gone into this moment; so much sacrifice. The performance was great; now everything rests with the judges.

Test Results

Athletes who perform well do not fear judges. Even in the case of judges who are reputed to be strict, the higher the standard such judges set, the more valuable and meaningful the results.

For the man or woman who honors God and His ways through the numerous trials of life, the mention of God as judge is not intimidating. Instead, it is encouraging, because God is good and faithful. For the righteous, His judgments mean justice and recompense. Abraham was correct in implying God, as "Judge of all the earth", would always "do right" (Genesis 18:25).

> *Now if anyone builds on this foundation with gold, silver, precious stones, wood, hay, straw, each one's work will become clear; for the Day will declare it, because it will be revealed by fire; and the fire will test each one's work, of what sort it is. If anyone's work which he has built on it endures, he will receive a reward.*
> 1 Corinthians 3:12-14

I remember many occasions when teachers or professors walked into our classroom with graded tests, quizzes or papers. Students who took their work seriously, prepared diligently and put forth their best effort in the exam or assignment, were always happy to receive their

---

Only God knows the full extent of any particular test's impact on our lives; therefore, *His* "grade" is the one that counts the most!

---

results. On the contrary, they who operated flippantly in their studies dreaded those moments. Generally, good students had a positive perception of teachers; scoffers and slackers criticized them.

Test results for many of the tests we go through are not limited to grades, certificates, diplomas, medals, doctor's reports or accolades. Awards and rewards, though appropriate in giving honor and recognition, can never fully represent the results of people's tests. The most significant and lasting consequences of passed tests are intangible. Only God knows the full extent of any particular test's impact on our lives; therefore, *His* "grade" is the one that counts the most!

Our Heavenly Father evaluates our hearts and efforts throughout the entire testing process. While we are being tested, God notes and appraises all our mindsets, thoughts, conversations, and actions. He determines test results by taking everything into account, not just the final outcome. The often-quoted saying, whose author remains unknown, is applicable:

"It doesn't matter whether you win or lose, it's how you play the game."

Whether we pass or fail tests, our objective must be to score high according to God's "test curve." He judges our performance with perfect fairness by His eternal and holy standards.

Test Results

I once watched an interview featuring a young man who had been training to become a Navy SEAL. He had just dropped out of the program. The interview was actually taking place near the bell dropouts rang to signify their withdrawal. This particular soldier had just rung the bell. He had failed to complete SEAL training.

In his remarks, the man passionately expressed serving his country as a Navy SEAL had been his lifelong dream. He felt physically and emotionally capable of completing the training. The needs of his family at that particular time required his presence and involvement. He said, "Family comes first, no matter what. They are my priority."

Having watched the performance of this particular soldier during some of the training that was filmed before the interview, I believe he was telling the truth. His commitment for his family superseded his desire to become a SEAL. His withdrawal may have appeared as a failure in the eyes of his instructors and comrades. In God's eyes, he passed a very significant test, that of laying down his own aspirations and dreams for the sake of his wife and children.

> In many cases, test results do not only appear *after* a test; they can be seen *throughout* the testing process.

~

The Next Test

In many cases, test results do not only appear *after* a test; they can be seen *throughout* the testing process. It is important to make the most out of every moment of our lives. Sometimes in our intense pursuit of end results, we may fail to take note of or enjoy the fruit of our efforts at various stages of our journey. Most of life's tests are multi-faceted. Every facet has its own challenges and rewards built in. We must learn to recognize and celebrate the positive results at every juncture.

> *I know that nothing is better for them than to rejoice and to do good in their lives, and also that every man should eat and drink and enjoy the good of all his labor – it is the gift of God.*
> Ecclesiastes 3:12-13

In many cases, test results do not only appear *after* a test; they can be seen *throughout* the testing process. For instance, splitting wood, which tests an individual's physical strength and endurance, is hard and potentially dangerous work. And yet, as Albert Einstein insightfully asserted, "People love chopping wood," because it is an activity in which "one immediately sees results." Indeed, wood-splitting progress is noticeable after the very first log is quartered.

Good results at different intervals of our trials encourage us to keep moving forward toward the finish line. Unfavorable results offer us the opportunity to make adjustments so we can do better. Either way, we make progress; either way, we grow.

One of my most favorite Scriptures is found in the fifth chapter of 1 Thessalonians:

> *Rejoice always, pray without ceasing, in everything give thanks; for this is the will of God in Christ Jesus for you.*
> 1 Thessalonians 5:16-18

I used to think it was impossible to live up to these commands and fulfill the will of God. How could I possibly be in constant communion with Him in prayer? How could I maintain a heart of joy and gratitude, when many of life's moments and seasons are saturated with hardship and adversity?

I began to find answers during times of testing. It started with thanksgiving. While under intense anguish and pain, I discovered there was always something for which I could thank God. I would discipline myself to list or speak out ten, twenty, or fifty things for which I was grateful. By the time I was done expressing thanks, the atmosphere would shift for the better. Layer by layer, fear, disappointment, frustration and heaviness lifted. Hope and peace emanated from my spirit, followed by the joy of the Lord. My attention and affection was focused

> Win or lose, succeed or fail; our trials hold the potential to draw us deeper into realms of intimacy with God.

on God. I learned how to lock into and remain conscious of His presence.

Over time, I grew in my ability to rejoice in God, commune with Him and give Him thanks in the midst of storms. My tests became catalysts for God's release of a greater grace over my life.

Win or lose, succeed or fail; our trials hold the potential to draw us deeper into realms of intimacy with God. Thanksgiving, prayer and joy will light our path to "the secret place of the Most High" (Psalm 91). The most favorable test results originate from that place!

~

All endorsements for *The Next Test* come from the leadership team of Valley Shore Assembly of God. Every individual and couple offering input regarding this work has modeled the principles I share. All of them face or have come through unthinkable calamity. At the very time this book is being completed, many of these co-laborers of mine are experiencing exceptionally strenuous tests. Their stories are riveting—*they* should be writing the book!

These precious friends have persevered through severe physical ailments, financial disasters, marital failures, the loss of loved ones, all forms of abuse, rejection, abandonment, demonic oppression, depression, family disasters, church splits, and the list goes on…

They do not bow to their circumstances. They do not seek pity or sympathy in their trials. Day after day, they walk in the presence of the Lord with an insatiable passion for more of Him. They fix their eyes on the face of Jesus and serve the Living God and His people with unconditional love, pure joy, and an unshakable sense of destiny.

I am honored to share life with these remarkable men and women. Together, we march forward to the heights and depths that unfold before us within the Kingdom of God. We celebrate our victories and learn from our failures. We give thanks for all results from all the tests we go through. Our eyes are fixed on Jesus and our ears to the sound of the Master, who one day as Supreme Judge will announce the test results we all live for:

Well done my good and faithful servants!

> *In this you greatly rejoice, though now for a little while, if need be, you have been grieved by various trials, that the genuineness of your faith, being much more precious than gold that perishes, though it is tested by fire, may be found to praise, honor, and glory at the revelation of Jesus Christ, whom having not seen you love.*
> 1 Peter 1:6-7

Epilogue:
The Next Test

~ Here is the test to find whether your mission on earth is finished. If you're alive, it isn't ~

Richard Bach

In our family and church, we are careful about the declarations we make. Recognizing the power of the tongue both to bless and curse, we continually hold each other accountable to speak words of life and truth. On one of the walls in our house, we have a large poster, on which we have handwritten the words of Ephesians 4:29:

> *Let no corrupt word proceed out of your mouth, but what is good for necessary edification, that it may impart grace to the hearers.*

I share this core value of ours as a disclaimer for my following statement:

You and I will be tested in the days ahead!

This is not a negative confession or a self-limiting prophesy; it is the truth. Until we complete our days on the earth, many tests await us. I have no idea what your next test or mine entails, but I am certain God's grace is sufficient to help us through.

In the most powerful and glorious Name of Jesus, I declare and decree blessing and promotion through each upcoming test we face. We will overcome by the "blood of the Lamb and by the word of [our] testimony" (Revelation 12:11), and God will be glorified through our lives in the heavens and on the earth, forever and ever!

Amen!

> *Behold, I have refined you, but not as silver; I have tested you in the furnace of affliction. For My own sake, for My own sake, I will do it; For how should My name be profaned? And I will not give My glory to another.* Isaiah 48:10-11

> *Because you have kept My command to persevere, I also will keep you from the hour of trial which shall come upon the whole world, to test those who dwell on the earth. Behold I am coming quickly! Hold fast what you have, that no one may take your crown.*
> Revelation 3:10-11

Contact Information:

Marios Ellinas
Valley Shore Assembly of God
36 Great Hammock Road
Old Saybrook, CT 06475

Email: maellinas@yahoo.com

To order more copies of this book, visit:

- www.amazon.com

Other books by Marios Ellinas:

Running to the Impossible (2008)

Warrior Material (2010)

www.ingramcontent.com/pod-product-compliance
Lightning Source LLC
Chambersburg PA
CBHW061650040426
42446CB00010B/1676